SHIFTING SHORES

SHIFTING SHORES

Rising Seas, Retreating Coastlines

JEFF HECHT

Charles Scribner's Sons • New York

Thanks to:

Rob Thieler, Duke University Program for the Study of Developed Shorelines, for valuable and extensive comments, finding photos, and other help above and beyond the call of duty.

Orrin H. Pilkey, Jr., James B. Duke Professor of Geology, Duke University; Stephen P. Leatherman, director of the Laboratory for Coastal Research, University of Maryland; Susan Halsey, New Jersey Marine Sciences Consortium; and Susan Scott, U.S. Army Corps of Engineers, for supplying information.

Clare Costello, for finding the right audience.

Carol Edwards, U.S. Geological Survey Photo Librarian; John C. Kraft, University of Delaware; Sergei Lebedeff, NASA Goddard Institute for Space Sciences; Mary Paden, World Resources Institute; Stephen Schneider, National Center for Atmospheric Research; and Edward J. Tarbuck, Illinois Central College, for helping find the right pictures.

Charles Scribner's Sons Books for Young Readers
Macmillan Publishing Company • 866 Third Avenue, New York, New York 10022
Collier Macmillan Canada, Inc.

Printed in the United States of America
First Edition   10 9 8 7 6 5 4 3 2 1

Library of Congress Cataloging-in-Publication Data
Hecht, Jeff.   Shifting shores / Jeff Hecht.—1st ed.   p.   cm.
Summary: Describes the various factors that change the shape of coastlines, including storms, natural erosion, and rising sea levels. Also discusses the future implications of these changes on coastal and low-lying centers of population and what can be done to protect the coastlines and slow the process of change.
    1. Coast changes—Juvenile literature.   [1. Coast changes.]   I. Title.
GB453.H43 1990   551.4′57—dc20   89–37812 CIP   AC
    ISBN 0–684–19087–7

To my parents,
who never thought I'd become a writer

Contents

1

The Coast Is Changing

The year I was eleven, my family moved to Longport, New Jersey, a small town at the south end of the island on which Atlantic City is located. Our house was a block and a half from the Atlantic Ocean, and I explored the beach shortly after we arrived. Soon, however, something else caught my attention. We went shopping at a small group of stores a few blocks down Atlantic Avenue, a broad street that runs the whole length of the island. Like other streets in Atlantic City, it is immortalized as a square on the Monopoly board. Just beyond the stores, Atlantic Avenue became much narrower.

I rode my bicycle down to investigate. The streets in Longport are numbered, starting from the south. We lived between Twenty-ninth and Thirtieth streets, and the stores were a few blocks south. At Twenty-second Street, the bay at the back of the island came up to one side of Atlantic Avenue, and the wide street became narrow, as if part of it had washed away. I could stand on the edge of the street and look down a sandy cliff into water only about 10 feet (3 meters) below.

Like other towns on the New Jersey shore, Longport was a summer resort, so many houses were vacant most of the year. It was a warm spring day. Most of the quiet old houses between Atlantic Avenue and the ocean were still shuttered, and there was no traffic. I rode farther down the street, wondering what was at the end of the island, but I had to stop just past Eleventh Street. The island ended there, and I looked down from a bluff onto sand and water.

What had happened to First through Tenth streets? They had been there when town planners laid the streets out in the late 1800s. Just after the turn of the century, the back of the island started thinning out at the southern end. The water broke through the island on a very high spring tide, leaving the south end as a small, low island. Soon the little island vanished, leaving Longport ten blocks shorter. Fifty years later, the only trace of the vanished land was the street names.

It was fun to have a beach at the end of the street. On summer days, I could walk down to play in the sand and swim. When the weather was cool, I could explore the beach, and in the evenings the night sky was dark and the stars bright.

Yet it was hard to forget the fate of the land at the end of the island. At night, if the windows were open, the sound of the waves was like the whispering of ghosts. When a storm drove waves over the wooden bulkhead at the end of the street, I realized that if the water came much higher, the ocean would be running down the street in front of my house.

My family moved away from the shore the following spring. I have never lived that close to the ocean again, but I have visited the seacoast many times. Each time I look carefully, I see signs of continuing change on the shifting shore. The rise and fall of the waves moves the sand, sweeping away yesterday's footprints and smoothing the beach. The water washes sand away from some places and adds it to other beaches. Oceanfront towns hide behind con-crete seawalls, built so that angry storms cannot wash houses away.

The news tells other stories of the changing sea. Storms destroy buildings on the water's edge. Hurricanes roar off the ocean, flooding low-lying coastal towns. Landslides on the California coast drop cliff-edge houses into the Pacific Ocean. The sea breaks through a Massachusetts island in a storm, splitting it in two. The slow, relentless rise of sea level threatens towns built a century ago along the shore. Historic lighthouses in North Carolina and New England are threatened by the ocean's digging away at their bases. Rising temperatures around the world threaten to raise sea level even faster.

Despite all this, many people think of the coast as unchanging. Tides rise and fall, but they seem to repeat the same pattern endlessly. Even scientists find it hard to measure average sea level changes that are much smaller than the tides. Most changes are slow, like the growth of trees, which we often don't notice at all. Storms make the most dramatic changes, but although they are part of nature, we tend to think they are unusual. One hurricane isn't enough to scare people from unsafe parts of the coast, a geologist told me, because that storm is an "act of God." It takes a second storm to teach the lesson.

This book tells about our shifting shores. It is an important story if you live on or near the coast, if you visit it, or if you care about this unique and fascinating region. It will become a more important story as time passes and the oceans continue to rise.

Already, much of New Orleans lies below sea level, and 40 to 60 square miles (100 to 150 square kilometers) of Louisiana marshland sink beneath the waters of the Gulf of Mexico each year. Hurricanes become more dangerous and life-threatening as the oceans rise, more and more people flock to fast-growing towns and cities along our coasts, and higher temperatures make the storms even stronger. This is a story that will become ever more vital through your lifetime.

The Appeal of the Coast

About three-quarters of the people in the United States live within 50 miles (80 kilometers) of an ocean or one of the Great Lakes. Most of our big cities are close to the shore. As Table 1–1 shows, only one of the country's twelve largest metropolitan areas is more than 50 miles from a coast. That exception is Dallas–Fort Worth, Texas, eighth on the list.

The United States is far from unique. The world's ten largest cities are (in order):

1. Tokyo and Yokohama (combined), Japan
2. Mexico City, Mexico
3. São Paolo, Brazil
4. New York City, United States
5. Seoul, South Korea
6. Osaka and Kyoto (combined), Japan
7. Buenos Aires, Argentina
8. Calcutta, India
9. Bombay, India
10. Rio de Janeiro, Brazil

Of those great metropolitan areas, only Mexico City is not near the ocean. Of the others, only Calcutta and Seoul do not border salt water. The trend holds for other countries as well. About 70 percent of Australians live in that nation's five largest coastal cities; the dry interior is sparsely populated.

Why are most of the world's biggest cities next to the ocean? Largely because they are seaports and centers of trade. Ships docked there, and industry grew near the seaports. People came to the cities looking for work, and companies started in the cities because they could find people to work in their factories.

When many of the world's biggest cities were founded, the sea was attractive because it was a road to adventure and other places.

TABLE 1–1: *The twelve largest metropolitan areas in the United States, with distances from the coast and elevations above sea level. (Population totals include suburbs and adjacent cities. Newark, New Jersey, for instance, is included in New York.)*

Major City	1986 Population	Location	Downtown elevation (ft)
New York	17,987,800	Atlantic coast	55
Los Angeles	13,074,800	Pacific coast	340
Chicago	8,116,100	Lake Michigan coast	595
San Francisco	5,877,800	Pacific coast	65
Philadelphia	5,832,600	along Delaware River, 50 miles from Atlantic Ocean	100
Detroit	4,600,700	between Lake Huron and Lake Erie	585
Boston	4,055,700	Atlantic coast	21
Dallas–Fort Worth	3,655,300	near Gulf of Mexico	435
Houston–Galveston	3,634,300	up to 40 miles from Gulf of Mexico	40
Washington, D.C.	3,563,000	along Potomac River, 20 miles from Chesapeake Bay	25
Miami	2,912,000	Atlantic coast	10
Cleveland	2,765,600	Lake Erie coast	660

For hundreds of years, restless young people looking for new experiences went to sea, sailing around the world. Today they are more likely to fly across the water, but the ocean has other attractions. Many of us think of the shore as a place to vacation or to relax for a day's outing, a pleasant place to play and forget about our daily chores. We may swim in the water, go fishing, waterskiing, or sailing, play in the sand, explore the coast, or just lie in the sun. Most people in the United States and other developed countries have leisure time, and many of them like to spend it along the shore.

The weather also makes the shore a pleasant place to live—most of the time. Go to the shore on a hot summer day and you may notice that it seems cooler near the water. It is, because land heats and cools much faster than the water, so in summer the ocean remains cool after the land has warmed. Sea breezes cool the shoreline in summer and warm it in the winter. On a summer afternoon, they cool the shore by 10° to 15° F (5° to 8° C). Visit the northeastern shore during the winter, and you will find less snow than just a few miles inland. Look at a national weather map and you can see the temperature differences between the shore and the middle of the country. The growing season is a few weeks longer along the shore because the last spring freeze is earlier and the first fall freeze is later.

The pleasant weather and the sense of romance of the sea have helped make the waterfront a popular place. Large housing and office developments line the shore downtown in coastal cities such as Boston. Summer and retirement homes and condominiums dot the Atlantic coast from Maine to Florida and the Gulf of Mexico coast from Florida to Texas. Movie stars and others spend millions of dollars for houses along the rugged California coast. Some people live near the shore year-round, commuting an hour or more to cities inland or farther along the coast. The prices of coastal property are soaring.

The Dark Side

The seacoast might sound like paradise on earth to a North Dakota farmer looking at a snow-covered winter landscape. Yet life along the shore has its drawbacks. No one over the age of five who has lived through a major coastal storm will ever forget the raging winds and pounding waves. If you haven't, you can see the drama in movies like *Key Largo* or *Condominium,* or when television news programs report on hurricanes. Even when the weather is calm, salt spray coats everything, making metal rust and windows murky. And the sea itself is rising, slowly eating away at the land.

Geologists tell us that sea level has been rising for over fifteen thousand years, since the great ice sheets that covered Europe and North America started melting at the end of the most recent Ice Age. They estimate that since that time, sea level has risen as much as 330 feet (100 meters). During the Ice Age people could walk from Siberia to Alaska—and they did, which is how the people we call Native Americans came to the Americas from Asia.

The biggest changes took place in the first few thousand years after the end of the Ice Age, but they continue today. We don't notice the water level rising because the change is tiny compared to the daily rise and fall of the tides. Typically, the ocean is a few feet (1 or 2 meters) higher at high tide than at low tide. The tides change once or twice a day. Scientists estimate that average sea level around the world rose about 4 inches (10 centimeters) in the last hundred years. Look at the difference, and you can see why it's hard to measure the change.

If you don't think that small a change could make much difference, visit one of the old resort towns along the East Coast that lost its beach years ago, like Monmouth Beach, New Jersey, shown in Figure 1–1. A hundred years ago, visitors came to enjoy the broad, flat beach. They built a town, complete with roads, railroads, summer houses, hotels, and shops. They picked home sites on sunny summer days, when they wanted to be close to the beach and the water. Later storms pushed the water too close to the buildings, so people built walls to protect their property. The slight rise in sea level helped the water go farther inland, so it hit the walls more and more often. Each time the waves hit the walls, they swept away some of the sand from the beach.

Year after year, the ocean took more of the sand, especially during storms, dumping it offshore. Today, in places like Marshfield,

FIGURE 1–1: *Condominium rising beside a seawall in Monmouth Beach, New Jersey. The sandy beach, which first lured people to the coastal town, is mostly gone. (Courtesy of Duke University Program for the Study of Developed Shorelines)*

Massachusetts, Sunny Isle, Florida, and Galveston, Texas, massive seawalls loom high above beaches. The beaches may seem wide at low tide, but at high tide little or no sand is visible, and the waves may hit the base of the wall. To reach what is left of the beach, you must climb a few steps to go over the seawall, then go down a 10- or 20-foot stairway to the sand.

Other resorts have saved their beaches, at least for a while, by taking sand from shallow water and pumping it onto the shore. Major resorts like Atlantic City and Miami Beach have spent millions of dollars pumping sand. Some of the sand soon washes away, but often enough stays to recreate the vanished beach—at least for a few years. Figure 1–2 shows Miami Beach before and after a fresh helping of sand.

Elsewhere around the world, land along the coast is vanishing. Scientists from the Woods Hole Oceanographic Institution in Massachusetts say that state is losing 65 acres of coastal property (0.26 square kilometer) each year to the rising Atlantic Ocean. With coastal property selling at about $1 million an acre, the losses add up quickly. Those losses pale compared to those in Louisiana, which each year loses about 40 square miles of coastal wetlands (25,000 acres, or 100 square kilometers) to the Gulf of Mexico.

Some of this land loss is gradual, day-by-day erosion of land along the waterline. Storms cause much more severe erosion when they hurl heavy waves against the shore. The most dramatic damage comes when hurricanes hit the coast, bringing heavy rains, high seas, and winds over 75 miles an hour (120 kilometers per hour). They can flood coastal lowlands and kill thousands of unprotected people. The worst coastal disaster on record was a 1970 storm that killed about 300,000 people in Bangladesh. The United States has been much luckier; the worst death toll from a single storm is the 6,000 people killed in 1900 when a hurricane hit Galveston, Texas, without warning.

Changes in Land and Sea

Sea level rises at about the same rate around the world. However, rising global sea level is not the only thing that changes the shoreline. The land itself rises and falls. In some parts of Greece where the land has been rising, archaeologists have found remains of twenty-five-hundred-year-old harbors bone dry and well above sea level. Off the coast of Spain, where the land has not risen to offset the rising sea, the remains of ancient coastal towns sit underwater offshore. Geologists drilling off the coast of British Columbia recently found remains of tree roots 310 feet (95 meters) under the

FIGURE 1–2: *Miami Beach before and after the beach was "replenished" by pumping sand from offshore in 1981. It cost $68 million to add new sand to 15 miles of beach. (Courtesy of Army Corps of Engineers)*

Pacific Ocean. Rocks now at the top of the Rocky Mountains were formed millions of years ago in shallow oceans.

The height of the land changes because the earth is not as rigid as we think. Motion of the earth's crust pushes some parts of the surface up and other parts down, forming mountains and valleys and causing earthquakes. Land once pushed down by the great weight of thick ice sheets continues to rise—like ice cubes floating to the top of water, but much more slowly. Sediments deposited at the mouths of rivers are settling. These changes differ from place to place, and so do changes in local sea level.

The first column in Table 1–2 shows how land is rising or falling compared to sea level along the United States coast. The changes are averaged over many years for each city and are given in millimeters per year. The minus signs show where the land is sinking and the sea is rising. The land really is sinking more slowly because global sea level is rising. Scientists had thought worldwide sea level was rising 1.2 millimeters a year, about an inch every twenty-one years. However, new research suggests sea level may be rising twice as fast, 2.4 millimeters per year. The second and third columns show how much land is rising or falling compared to some constant point, not to the rising sea.

The changes may seem small, but over the long term they add up. If the sea continues rising 0.11 inch (2.7 millimeters) a year compared to New York City, the water level will rise 11 inches (27 centimeters) in one hundred years, and over 9 feet (2.7 meters) in a thousand years.

You may think you need not worry about a change that will take a thousand years, but it won't really take that long. As we will see later, people are making the earth's climate warmer, and that will make sea level rise faster in the future. Scientists are not sure how much sea level will rise, but they say that the average could increase by 1.6 to 11.5 feet (0.5 to 3.5 meters) by the year 2100. That spells

TABLE 1–2: *Rise or fall of selected North American coastal cities in millimeters per year (1 millimeter is 1/25 of an inch). Scientists estimate local changes in sea level, then try to subtract global changes in sea level to get true change in altitude of the land. Because scientists are not sure if global sea level is rising 1.2 or 2.4 millimeters a year, the table shows changes in land level for both values.*

	Rise (+) or fall (−) (mm/year)		
City	Compared to local sea level	Local land change if global sea level rises 1.2 mm/yr	Local land change if global sea level rises 2.4 mm/yr
Boston, Massachusetts	− 2.2	− 1.0	0.2
Providence, Rhode Island	− 1.7	− 0.5	0.7
New York, New York	− 2.7	− 1.5	− 0.3
Atlantic City, New Jersey	− 4.1	− 2.9	− 1.7
Baltimore, Maryland	− 3.2	− 2.0	− 0.8
Philadelphia, Pennsylvania	− 2.6	− 1.4	− 0.2
Hampton Roads, Virginia	− 4.3	− 3.1	− 1.9
Wilmington, North Carolina	− 1.8	− 0.6	0.6
Charleston, South Carolina	− 3.4	− 2.2	− 1.0
Miami Beach, Florida	− 2.3	− 1.1	0.1
Grand Isle, Louisiana	− 10.1	− 8.9	− 7.7
Galveston, Texas	− 6.3	− 5.1	− 3.9
San Diego, California	− 0.8	0.4	1.6
Los Angeles, California	− 0.8	0.4	1.6
San Francisco, California	− 1.3	− 0.1	1.1
Seattle, Washington	− 2.0	− 0.8	0.4
Juneau, Alaska	12.6	13.8	15.0
Skagway, Alaska	18.3	19.5	20.7

big trouble for low-lying cities such as Miami and New Orleans—parts of New Orleans already are below sea level.

As sea level rises, the ocean will cover lowlands along the shore. How far the water moves inland depends on the slope of the land.

The flatter the land, the farther inland the sea will come, as shown in Figure 1–3. Beaches are flat, so geologists estimate that a 1-inch (2.5 centimeters) rise in sea level will make the coast retreat inland 8.3 feet (2.5 meters)—or more in some areas. Coastal lands are flat from New York to Texas, so shores there will "retreat" far inland as the sea rises. Along the Pacific coast, where most coastal land is steep, much larger rises in sea level will not change the maps in a big way.

The rising water will continually erode and reshape natural coastlines. Geologists have learned that the ocean has enough power to move whole islands. As the water rises, the waves push sandy islands back toward the mainland. It takes many years, but eventually the whole island will have moved so far that shells left on the inland shore will reappear on the ocean side of the island.

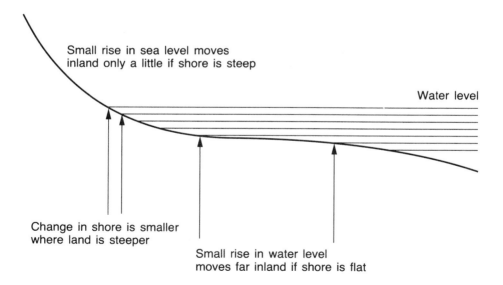

FIGURE 1–3: *As sea level rises, it submerges land near the shore. The flatter the land, the farther inland the sea moves.*

The Threat of Rising Sea Level

As we develop the coast, we raise the stakes in the battle against increasing sea level. We have invested hundreds of billions of dollars in coastal real estate and buildings, and all that is at risk as the sea creeps higher. People who live near the shore face a growing risk from severe storms, a threat eased—but not avoided—by satellites that give us early warning of oncoming hurricanes. The threat goes beyond resorts to a long list of major coastal cities around the world. It is most severe in developing countries, particularly low-lying Bangladesh.

Ironically, the love for the ocean that drives us to the shore also threatens to destroy coastal beaches and wetlands. Left to itself, nature can adjust, forming new beaches and wetlands on what is now dry ground inland. However, "nature" can be crowded out of existence if it is trapped between developed areas and the rising sea. You can find little that is natural on islands armored with massive seawalls; stand on the beach and the concrete wall dominates your view.

What can be done about coastal erosion? Someday we may learn how to control climate and to stop heating the planet, but for now we must live with the reality of rising sea level. Engineers can defend coastal cities with seawalls and other structures, and they can add sand to restore beaches temporarily. However, as the oceans continue to rise, these structures must get bigger and more costly. Many coastal geologists believe a better solution would be a planned retreat from the threatened areas. They say that natural processes will move beaches and wetlands inland along with the shore, and that people should not build large and expensive structures in threatened areas.

Look very far ahead, and you can see some very scary possibilities. If we continue warming the earth, we might melt the great ice sheets that cover Antarctica and Greenland. Scientists estimate that water would make the oceans 200 to 230 feet (60 to 70 meters) deeper. No engineering barriers could protect our coasts from that much water. Most of Florida, Louisiana, and Delaware would be underwater. The sea would come far inland along much of the eastern coast. Elsewhere around the world, low-lying countries like the Netherlands might be submerged. The changes would force our descendants to draw new maps of the world.

2

The Ocean and the Shore

The shore is the border between land and sea. Except in the steepest, rockiest regions, it is a broad and changing border because the water is always moving. The line between water and land changes from minute to minute as waves rise and fall. The tides rise and fall once or twice a day, moving the waterline up and down the beach. Storms can drive big waves across what is normally dry land.

The sea changes so much that you cannot mark the border between land and water with a narrow line. The shoreline is drawn with a broad brush, not a fine pen. The whole gently sloping, natural beach is one broad shoreline, extending both above and below the waterline. Wade into the water at low tide, and you can feel sand under your feet. This is the underwater part of the beach. The sand that stays dry at high tide also is part of the beach, where wind and waves can drive the water during storms.

The shape of the coast depends on both the earth and the water. The sea shatters rocks into pebbles and sand, but the harder the rock, the longer this process takes. If the water meets the land where it slopes gently, it forms broad beaches and chains of long, thin, sandy islands. If the land is mountainous, the sea forms a line

16

of cliffs with the ocean and piles of rocky rubble at their base. To understand the forces that shape the land and the sea, we must look at the structure of the earth's crust.

The Earth's Surface

Many maps make the earth's surface look too simple, as if it is either land or water. Look at a physical, or contour, map, and you can see that the land is made up of mountains and plains, some high in altitude, others only a little above sea level. Take away the water in Figure 2–1, and you can see that the ocean bottom has its own mountains, valleys, plains, and plateaus. The Hawaiian Islands are the tops of sea-bottom mountains, sticking out of the water; they rise higher from the ocean bottom than Mt. Everest rises from sea level. The ocean basins are broad, flat plains, averaging about 2.5 to 3.7 miles (4 to 6 kilometers) below sea level. A few valleys, called "trenches" or "troughs," go deeper, up to 6.8 miles (11 kilometers) below the sea level.

Geologists say the earth's surface is made of continental and oceanic crust. Thin oceanic crust covers the bottoms of the ocean basins. Thick continental crust rises far above the bottom of the ocean basins. You can see the difference clearly on our map of the dry earth.

The earth has more water than it needs to fill the ocean basins. Figure 2–1 shows how the extra water spills onto the lower edges of the continental crust. Geologists call those submerged edges of the continents the "continental shelf." They view the edge of the continental shelf rather than the coastline as the true edge of the continent. The border between continental shelf and ocean bottom is called the "continental slope," which is not as steep as it looks here. Typically the continental shelf is covered by 400 feet (130 meters) or less of water, while 2 miles (3.2 kilometers) or more of water cover the ocean basins.

FIGURE 2–1: *The earth without its oceans. Continental crust extends beyond the shoreline, forming submerged continental shelves. The deep areas are ocean basins. (World Ocean Floor by Bruce C. Heezen and Marie Tharp, copyright 1977, Marie Tharp, reproduced by permission)*

Oceans cover 70.8 percent of the earth's surface, and only 29.2 percent is dry land. However, 5 percent of the earth's surface is shallow sea covering the continental shelf. The width of the continental shelf varies greatly around the globe. It is narrow—often about 20 miles (32 kilometers) wide—where land rises steeply, like the western coasts of North and South America. It is much broader along flat coasts, such as the eastern coast of North America, where in many places it is 100 miles (160 kilometers) wide.

Some large seas are only shallow water. Only continental shelf separates England, Scotland, and Ireland from the European mainland. In fact, the entire North Sea covers continental shelf and averages only 308 feet (94 meters) deep. The Baltic Sea averages only 180 feet (55 meters) deep. Similarly, the Bering Strait that separates Alaska from Siberia is only shallow water on a continental shelf that stretches from Alaska to Siberia without interruption. If sea level was 130 feet (40 meters) lower, North America and Asia would be connected. Hudson Bay in Canada also is shallow water on continental crust, but the Mediterranean Sea, the Gulf of Mexico, the Gulf of California, and the Caribbean Sea all are deep, with bottoms at least partly covered by ocean crust.

The way oceans spill onto the continents means that a small change in sea level could make large changes to our maps. If average sea level dropped just 1 percent, or 125 feet (38 meters), it would expose many now-submerged regions around the globe. The Bering Strait would dry up, linking Alaska with Siberia. The eastern coast of the United States would extend many miles farther into the Atlantic, and islands like Long Island, Martha's Vineyard, and Nantucket would become part of the mainland. Raising sea level by the same amount would submerge southern Florida and southern Louisiana. Even larger changes, we shall see, have been known to happen.

Changes in Sea Level

One of the first lessons of geology is that the earth changes. We don't see the changes because they are very slow in human terms. Continents may move an inch (2 or 3 centimeters) a year, but that adds up over millions of years. Rocks wear very slowly, but gradually they are worn away into sand and dirt that wash down rivers to the sea. There they form sediments, which build up over many years and are pressed into rocks. In time, those new rocks may be thrust up into mountains that again are worn down by the geological cycle.

Nineteenth-century scientists knew none of this when they started finding fossils. They were amazed to find remains of fish and other sea creatures on dry land. They first thought those fossils were leftovers from the biblical flood, but eventually they realized that oceans long ago covered areas that are now land. One hundred million years ago, for example, a shallow sea covered central North America, separating what are now the eastern and western parts of the continent. Most of Europe, the west coast of North America, and much of central Africa also were underwater. Sea level may have been higher, the land lower, or both.

Sea level can rise and fall for many reasons. Scientists believe that the earth is not gaining or losing much water, and they know that oceans have covered much of the planet for billions of years. However, it would not take much change to redraw the map. Adding just 5 percent more water would raise sea level about 620 feet (190 meters), enough to flood most of the Amazon basin in South America, make St. Louis and Birmingham, Alabama, into seaports, and submerge huge areas in the Soviet Union.

All the earth's water is not in the oceans, as shown in Table 2–1. Draining all the lakes and rivers, or getting all the rain out of the clouds, would do little to change sea level. However, there are about 6 million cubic miles (25 million cubic kilometers) of ice on

TABLE 2–1: *Where the earth stores its water*

Place	Percentage
Oceans and seas	97.29
Ice	2.09
Underground	0.6054
Fresh lakes and rivers	0.0144
Water vapor in air	0.00094
Living things	0.00004

the earth, most of it covering Antarctica and Greenland. If all that ice melted, the water would raise sea level about a couple of hundred feet (60 or 70 meters). At the peak of the last ice age, eighteen thousand years ago, thick ice sheets covered northern Europe and North America. Nearly three times more water was frozen in polar ice than today. The extra water came from the oceans, so sea level was about 330 feet (100 meters) lower.

Adding that much water to or subtracting it from the oceans would dramatically change the outlines of the continents. Figure 2–2 shows one scientist's estimates of how one part of the coast of the eastern United States has retreated since the Ice Age—and how much more the land would be flooded if the earth grew warm enough to melt the rest of the ice.

It is not just melting ice that makes sea level rise as the world warms. Above 39° F (4° C), water expands as it warms. The change is small, but the ocean is so big that the expansion causes some of the change we see in global sea level.

Ice sheets naturally form and melt in thousands of years, which is rapid on a geological time scale. Over millions of years, the sizes of the ocean basins can change, and that changes how much water they can hold. Erosion washes bits of rock and soil from the land into the water. Volcanic eruptions create island chains. The sea floor spreads and contracts as the continents move slowly around the globe. Heating or cooling can raise or lower the bottoms of ocean basins. If the ocean basins grow, the water retreats from the edges of the continents; if the basins shrink, they force water onto the continental shelf.

Changes in the Land

All of the earth's crust is caught up in a process called "plate tectonics." The crust is broken up into giant chunks, or "plates," which move slowly around the globe. Some plates are gigantic, in-

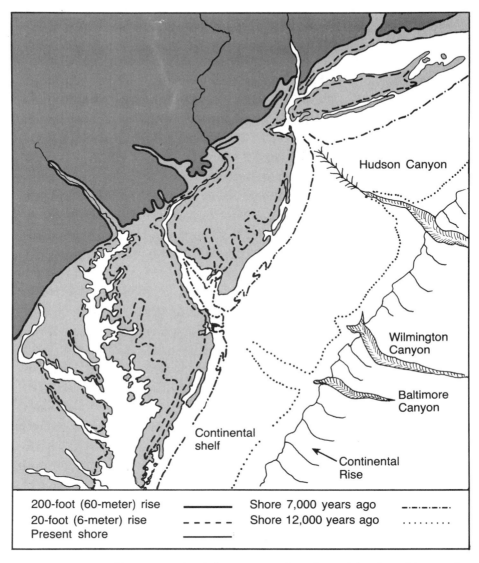

Hudson Canyon

Wilmington
Canyon

Baltimore
Canyon

Continental
shelf

Continental
Rise

200-foot (60-meter) rise	———————	Shore 7,000 years ago	—·—·—·—·—
20-foot (6-meter) rise	- - - - -	Shore 12,000 years ago	·········
Present shore	———————		

FIGURE 2–2: *Changes in the Atlantic coast from Long Island to Chesapeake Bay caused by changing sea level. The outer lines show the shore 12,000 years ago, shortly after the end of the last ice age, and about 7,000 years ago, after most of the ice had melted. Lines inside the present coast show how far the shoreline would retreat if sea level rose 20 feet (6 meters) and if present ice caps melted completely, raising sea level about 200 feet (60 meters). (Courtesy of John C. Kraft, University of Delaware)*

cluding continents and surrounding ocean areas such as North America, South America, and Australia. Others are much smaller pieces of continental or ocean crust.

The plates themselves change. New ocean crust forms along ridges that run down the middle of the ocean. Old plates collide, and one pushes over another. Plates can split or weld together. Volcanoes form in active zones, where old crust is being forced down into the earth or where new crust is forming.

Plate collisions crumble the crust to form mountains. The western mountains of North and South America formed as the continents moved over the crust of the Pacific Ocean. The world's tallest mountains, the Himalayas, formed when India, once a small, separate continent, collided with the rest of Asia. India is still pushing north, and the mountains are still rising. Colliding plates can squeeze oceans out of existence.

Over time, erosion wears down mountains. Water, weather, and wind break the rock into tiny pieces that wash off the land along with plant debris, then flow down rivers. The rivers drop their loads of tiny sediment particles on lowlands during floods, or at their mouths where they meet the oceans. These sediments build new land. Sediment from the Mississippi River built much of Louisiana. Eventually, the sediments turn into sedimentary rock, which plate collisions can thrust into high mountains. Rocks now high in the Rocky Mountains were formed millions of years ago in shallow seas.

Continents can split apart to form oceans. The Atlantic Ocean started as a crack that ran through a great continent, but grew over millions of years into the large ocean that separates the Americas from Europe and Africa. Today's Red Sea is a young ocean, which is splitting Arabia from Africa.

Our lifetimes are too short to see plate tectonics make mountains or oceans, but we can see tectonic forces move the land up and down. Sometimes the changes are sudden, such as during an earthquake; other times they are gradual. The west coast of North America is rising as it pushes over the old crust of the Pacific Ocean.

Other things can make land rise and fall, too. The most important are aftereffects of melted ice sheets. The weight of the massive ice sheets pushed down the land they covered. Once the ice was removed, the continents started rising back up, just as ice cubes pushed below the surface of water might, but much more slowly. Along the west coast of British Columbia, some areas rose 330 feet (100 meters) in about fifteen hundred years when ice sheets melted ten thousand years ago. Eastern Canada and Alaska are still "rebounding" from the melting of the ice sheets, although at a much slower pace.

Many other things can make land rise and fall locally. People can make the land sink if they pump oil or gas from underground. The earth gradually settles, filling in spots once filled by the thick, gooey oil or the highly compressed gas. The changes can be large. Some areas near Long Beach, California, sank 0.5 to 8 feet (0.15 to 2.5 meters) between 1921 and 1948 as oil was pumped out of a large field.

Lakes and Rivers

The same factors that influence sea level can change the levels of lakes, but they work on a different scale. The oceans contain the same amount of water year to year, but the amount of water in a lake can vary from season to season. Over many years, lake sizes vary as climate changes. Great Salt Lake is all that remains of a much larger lake that covered much of the Utah basin thousands of years ago, when the area was wetter.

An arm of the ocean can dry up if it is cut off from the rest of the sea. This happened a few million years ago when Africa collided with the southern end of Europe, blocking the Mediterranean Sea from the rest of the ocean. Water evaporated faster than it entered, and gradually the Mediterranean dried out, leaving thick sheets of salt. Later, the Atlantic Ocean broke through the western barrier, forming the Strait of Gibraltar as water poured into the dry seabed. Water still enters the Mediterranean from the Atlantic because water evaporates from the sea faster than it enters from the surrounding land.

If you live near a river, you can see its yearly cycle. A river changes more than a lake because its water continually flows away and must always be replenished. In the spring, when snow is melting and rains are usually heaviest, the river runs the highest. Sometimes it overflows its banks, flooding land next to it. The river level drops during summer because there is less rain.

The Climate Connection

You might think that climate is much more important in shaping the shores of lakes and rivers than in changing seacoasts. Rainfall does not change sea level directly, but temperature is part of climate, and it has a very important effect on sea level. Ice sheets grow if it gets colder and shrink if it gets warmer. As we have seen, those changes in ice cover have a very strong effect on sea level.

Thirty years ago, scientists worried about the return of the great ice sheets that covered Europe and North America. Today they believe that people are making the earth warmer. Careful measurements show slight increases in average temperature around the world during the last hundred years. We know that people are adding carbon dioxide and other gases to the air and that those gases can trap energy to make the planet warmer, in ways we will explain in Chapter 9. This may prevent a return of the ice age, but it brings other problems. The warmer temperatures make the oceans rise by melting ice and expanding the volume of water already in the oceans.

Because the continents rise and fall, it is very hard to measure exactly how much average sea level is changing around the world. For several years, scientists believed sea level was rising about 0.047 inch (1.2 millimeters) a year. However, new measurements suggest the change may be twice as large, 0.094 inch (2.4 millimeters) a year. By the year 2100, scientists expect sea level to rise 1.6 to 11.5 feet (0.5 to 3.5 meters). That threatens shores around the world and puts low-lying cities like Miami and New Orleans in serious danger. If temperatures continue rising, they might melt more ice. If the earth gets warm enough to melt the ice that covers Greenland and Antarctica, sea level would rise about 200 feet (60 to 70 meters). That would push the coast far inland in some areas, as shown in Figure 2–2.

3

Building Beaches

When we think of the shore, we usually think of sandy beaches, but sand is not all you find along the water. In some places, rocks or cliffs line the shore. Elsewhere, mud flats or marshes mark the border between land and sea. Often, you can walk from one zone to another, such as from a sandy beach to rocky bluffs sticking out into the water.

Natural forces create many types of shore. The type depends on the local geology. Where sand is abundant and the land is flat, broad, sandy beaches face the waves. The United States has one of the world's longest stretches of flat, sandy beaches, which are the usual shoreline from Long Island, New York, down the Atlantic coast, around Florida, and all the way to the southern tip of Texas. In flat areas protected from strong waves, such as the back sides of islands, you can find mud flats or broad, flat marshes, "wetlands" partly covered by water that rises and falls with the gentle tides. Where mountains rise steeply from the sea along the California and Oregon coasts, there is little or no beach. Cliffs form where the sea meets hills of soft rock, sand, or soil in Cape Cod or California.

Making Sand

Sand is the usual stuff of beaches and shores. You usually can find some even at the base of rugged ocean cliffs. Look closely at the sand, and you will see that each grain is a tiny rock. The finer the sand, the smaller the rocks. Grains of very fine sand are so small you may need a magnifying glass to see them, but they are still rocks.

Nature makes sand by breaking rocks into pieces. You would use a hammer, but nature's hammers are wind, water, and weather. Cracks form as rocks heat and cool in the sun. Water works its way into the cracks, pushing them open as it warms and cools, and especially when it gets cold enough to freeze. Ocean waves pound rocks along the shore and throw them against each other, chipping off fragments that become sand. Slowly, nature wears down rocks all over the world, high in the mountains as well as along the shore. Some sand formed inland ends up in deserts, but rivers carry much of it to the sea, where currents carry it along the shore.

Look carefully at riverbeds, and you can find sand. In spring, streams run high and the sand may be washed far downstream, to be dropped where the river runs slowly. It may be trapped behind rocks or at the base of a waterfall. Some of the smoothest, finest sand I have ever seen is at the base of a dam on the Saco River in Maine. Eventually, that sand will wash down the river to the Atlantic Ocean and cover beaches.

Beaches need sand just as lakes and rivers need water. The steady pounding of ocean waves makes sand, but storms and strong currents wash some away. Some sand is buried and lost offshore. Rivers bring fresh sand to the ocean, and currents push it along the shore. The soft sand from the Saco River ends up on the sandy beaches of southern Maine. The Los Angeles, San Gabriel, and Santa Ana rivers bring sand from the mountains around Los Angeles to form the sandy beaches that line the nearby coast. Sand along the coasts of Washington and Oregon comes from the Columbia River. Sand

TABLE 3–1: *Geological classification of sand sizes*

Size class	Diameter (mm)	Diameter (in)	Typical beach slope
Boulders	over 256	over 10	—
Cobbles	64–256	2.5–10	24°
Pebbles	4–64	0.16–2.5	17°
Granules	2–4	0.08–0.16	11°
Very coarse sand	1–2	0.04–0.08	9°
Coarse sand	1/2–1	0.02–0.04	7°
Medium sand	1/4–1/2	0.01–0.02	5°
Fine sand	1/8–1/4	0.005–0.01	3°
Very fine sand	1/16–1/8	0.0025–0.005	1°
Silt	1/256–1/16	0.00015–0.0025	—
Clay	under 1/256	under 0.00015	—

also washes from cliffs and dunes along the shore. The people who live along those cliffs and dunes see this as erosion, but the same sand will help build or maintain a beach elsewhere along the shore.

The way sand moves along the shore and builds beaches depends on its size and texture. Size and texture, in turn, depend on the forces that make the sand and the waves that hit the beach. Ocean waves tend to pound sand into finer and finer grains, but they also can wash the finer grains away. Visit many beaches, and you will find that the type of sand can differ greatly.

To geologists, grains of sand, pebbles, boulders, and even mud are just pieces of rock. These scientists separate them by size, as shown in Table 3–1. Piles of anything from boulders to granules—0.08 inch (2 millimeters) or more in diameter—are "gravel." Silt and clay make mud (the particles are too small to feel grainy to your fingers). Anything between mud and gravel is sand, and even gravel can make a beach. Along rocky coasts, you can find beaches cov-

FIGURE 3–1: *Pacific Ocean surf pounds stones on a "cobble" beach north of San Diego.*

ered with rounded stones like overgrown grains of sand, as shown in Figure 3–1.

The finer the sand, the flatter the beach. Waves can spread fine sand smoothly around a beach, but they can't move rocks as easily, so rocky beaches have steeper slopes. Table 3–1 shows typical slopes for beaches made of various sizes of rock and sand.

Size is not all that differs among sand particles. Sand is made of rock, but there are many types of rock. You can see the difference if you look closely at particles of coarse sand. The most common mineral in sand is quartz, which is clear or milky white and comes from granite, one of the most common rocks. White quartz sand is melted to make glass. Sand also contains feldspar, mica, and other rocks. Mica is the easiest to identify, because it forms tiny, flat flakes. Feldspar, like quartz, comes from granite. Mixed with the rock fragments are pieces of seashells and coral, which are hard to identify in fine sand. The sea will add anything it can find to the beach. Australian geologist Eric C. F. Bird wrote that "the most unusual beach material" he had seen was pieces of ceramic pipe washed up near a pipe factory on Brownsea Island in Poole Harbor in Dorset, England.

The color of sand depends on the rocks it contains. We usually think of sand as white, or "sand"-colored light brown, which is tinted by rustlike iron impurities. However, weathering of dark rocks on volcanic islands, such as Hawaii, can produce black-sand beaches. Other tropical beaches, including those in southern Florida, are white with shell fragments.

Beach Structures

You may think of the beach only as the sand wet by ocean waves, where you play or lie in the sun. What geologists call the beach extends farther, as shown in Figure 3–2. The inland or upland end of the beach is a line of sand dunes or bluffs. Waves can reach them in a heavy storm, but on a calm day they look like dry land, and many people have built houses on them. The "back shore" is a flat region between the dunes and the steeper zone, called the "foreshore," where the tides normally rise and fall. The level areas on the back shore and foreshore, where sunbathers often lie, are called "berms." The slope levels off at the base of the foreshore, slightly below the level of low tide, which is called the "terrace," or "runnel." This is the zone where waves break, forming surf, and where people stand in the water. Sometimes sand ridges appear at low-tide level in this flat region. Sandbars are ridges farther out, where the water becomes shallow. The beach proper extends all the way from the back shore to the outer edge of the terrace. Sand extends even farther offshore and inland, and sometimes storms can move sand between the beach and those regions.

These patterns appear on beaches around the world, although their shapes and sizes vary. They are formed by the action of the ocean on the local landscape. Storms can take sand from the back shore, dumping some sand in the water and making the foreshore slope gentler. After the storm, gentle waves push the sand back onto the shore, rebuilding the back shore.

In many places, storms are more common in the winter than in the summer, so the winter beach is steeper and narrower than the summer beach. The difference can be startling if you are not prepared for it. In Carmel, California, the summer beach is over 200 feet (60 meters) wide, but storms make the beach retreat in the fall, and by January or February the beach is almost gone. Yet each year the summer beach returns as gentler waves bring the sand back from where it spent the winter offshore.

Usually, beaches curve only slightly, so waves break parallel to the waterline. However, this is only on the average because wave

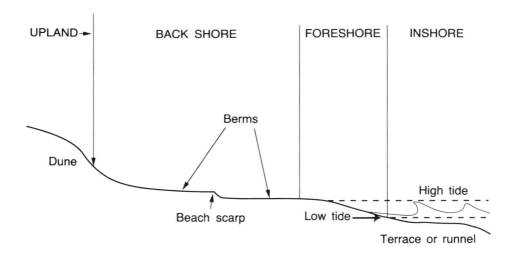

FIGURE 3–2: *The structure of a beach, viewed from the side, from the inland dunes to the outer zones underwater.*

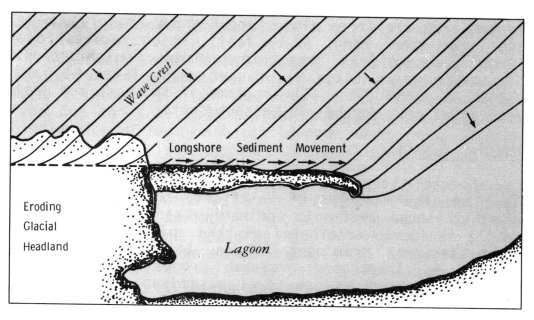

FIGURE 3–3: *Current flowing along the shore carries sand with it, forming a coastal "spit," a narrow sandy peninsula that looks like an island but is connected to the mainland. This example, Sandy Neck, is on Cape Cod in Massachusetts. (Courtesy of Stephen Leatherman, University of Maryland)*

direction changes with the wind. Beach shape also depends on what lies underwater offshore because waves extend under the surface. Rocks and other underwater features can bend waves, "focusing" them on some places on shore.

Ocean currents move sand along the shore and sometimes shape the coast into odd forms. In some places, they form "spits" or "cusps" of sand that project out into the ocean, as shown in Figure 3–3. This happens when waves moving along the coast pick up sand and carry it beyond the end of an island or straight strip of coast. As the current turns, it drops the sand, gradually building a spit or cusp. Some of these features are small and don't last long enough to make it onto the map, but you can find others if you look at detailed maps. Two of the larger examples are the tip of Cape Cod, in Massachusetts, and Sandy Hook, New Jersey, just south of New York

City. Both were formed by currents that collected sand as they flowed north along sandy coasts. Spits form many beaches along the West Coast.

Currents continually reshape the shore, taking sand from one place to another. In some places they shift from season to season. Along the Oregon shore, winter winds push sand north, while summer waves push it south. The winter storms are stronger, pushing more sand north than goes south in the summer.

The currents spread sand from river mouths to beaches along the shore. They also take sand from coastal bluffs and dunes and push it up and down the shore, the way a gentle wave will spread the remains of a sand castle it has swept over. This new sand builds beaches, spits, and cusps along the shore. The Provincetown area at the north tip of Cape Cod and Monomoy Island at the south did not exist fifteen thousand years ago, after melting glaciers dropped the sand and rock that formed the Cape. Strong Atlantic Ocean waves carried sand north and south from the central part of the Cape to form them. The new land came at the expense of erosion of the bluffs in the middle of the Cape.

Waves and currents tend to make a sandy shoreline smooth and gently curving, but they, too, are affected by many other forces. The shape of the land may form capes that reach out into the sea. Rocks along the shore or underwater affect current flow. Tidal range, land slope, climate, vegetation, local land movement, and sand texture all affect the shape of a beach.

Barrier Islands

If you live along the West Coast, or near the Great Lakes, the beaches you visit are part of the mainland. If you live along the East Coast between New Jersey and Texas, you probably visit island beaches. The sandy islands are long and narrow, and they run parallel to the mainland shore. Geologists call them "barrier islands," because they form barriers that protect the mainland from strong ocean waves. Shallow lagoons separate them from the mainland, although in some places the lagoons are shallow marshes that may not show on maps. The Intracoastal Waterway runs through these lagoons (and some man-made canals) from New Jersey to Texas.

The United States is home to the world's longest string of barrier islands, which lie along 47 percent of the U.S. coastline. About three hundred barrier islands run from New Jersey down to Florida and around the Gulf of Mexico to the Mexican border with Texas.

Barrier islands form where land is nearly flat along the coast. You might think of them as overgrown sandbars. Figure 3–4 shows their structure. Tides rise and fall on a flat, level beach. Inland are dunes, which are covered with plants and trees on undeveloped islands. They are the island's backbone, a ridge of sand that storms and winds have pushed above the high-water line. Behind the dunes are marshes and a low-lying bay or lagoon, filled with salt water. Beyond that is the mainland.

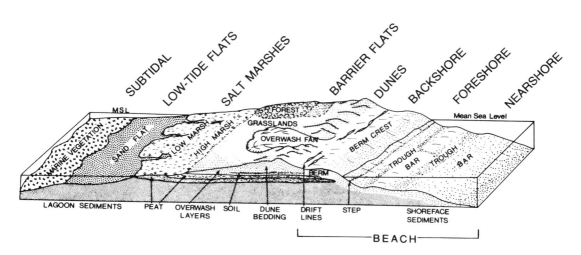

FIGURE 3–4: *Side view across an undeveloped barrier island. (Courtesy of Paul J. Godfrey, University of Massachusetts, Amherst, and Oceanus)*

Like their smaller cousins, sandbars, barrier islands can be moved by water. Because they are larger, they move more slowly, in years rather than in a season. However, as sea level rises, it pushes the whole barrier-island sand pile inland. You might think of the island—and the watery lagoon or marsh behind it—as riding on the edge of the ocean.

Some barrier islands are very long. Except when tides are unusually high in a storm, Mustang and Padre islands along the Texas coast form a single barrier island 130 miles (209 kilometers) long. Most barrier islands are much shorter, because more water flows from the land into the lagoons than it does in dry south Texas. Islands are separated by inlets that connect the sea with the lagoons behind them. Geologists say that inlets can move because old ones can fill up with sand while strong tides and storms can cut new ones.

True barrier islands are built only of sand. The Florida Keys look like barrier islands, but they are not true barrier islands because they are built on coral reefs, which makes them more stable.

Tidal Mud Flats and Marshes

Barrier beaches grow where ocean waves rise over low-lying land. In back of a barrier island, or in bays protected from the full force of ocean waves, seawater rises and falls in tidal flats and marshes. Tidal flats, wide, smooth areas with little obvious plant growth, are covered with water at high tide and exposed at low tide. Marshes are flat areas covered with marsh grass or other plants—seaside swamps that we call wetlands. Back from the shore, in Louisiana and the Florida Everglades, the water is fresh, but along the ocean marshes contain salt water.

The water level in a salt marsh rises and falls with the tide. You might see mud under the grass at low tide, and water at high tide. Heavy tides and waves destroy delicate wetlands plants, so marshes form only where protected from the full force of the waves. Marshes form between barrier islands and the mainland, where the island protects them. They also form in protected bays and harbors, such as those on the side of Cape Cod facing inward.

Natural marshes do not have sharp borders, and you can pass through one on a road without realizing it. If you ride to a barrier island beach, watch for tall grass near the shore. That may be a salt- or freshwater marsh. Marshes can be much broader than barrier islands, and in some places—including Florida, Louisiana, New Jersey, North Carolina, and South Carolina—they extend for many miles inland.

Like other wetlands, marshes have an important role in coastal ecology. They are fertile nesting grounds for many birds and nurture sea life as well. Federal laws now protect them, but for many years people thought they were useful only for breeding mosquitoes and dumping garbage. Parts of many coastal cities were built on filled-in wetlands.

Cliffs and Rocky Coasts

People who grow up on the East Coast of the United States think of the coast as a broad, flat plain meeting the sea at a barrier island or other sandy beach. However, in much of Maine, the West Coast, Hawaii, or southern Alaska, people grow up with a different shore, where breakers crash against rocks and beaches are narrow strips between the ocean and cliffs. The broad flat beaches of the Los Angeles area are exceptions. The cliff shown in Figure 3–5 at Dana Point, California—between Los Angeles and San Diego—is more typical. Farther north, along the spectacular Pacific Coast Highway north of San Luis Obispo, some cliffs rise straight from the Pacific.

The height of a cliff depends on the strength of the dirt or rock that makes it up. Low cliffs or bluffs form where the hills are made of weak material. Walk along the Cape Cod National Seashore, and

FIGURE 3–5: *Cliffs like this one in Dana Point, California, are common on the West Coast. Note the house perched on the cliff, with its deck hanging out over the rocks. The sandy beach is at the base of another hill.*

you will find cliffs of sand and gravel 50 to over 150 feet (15 to over 45 meters) high. Strong Atlantic waves erode about 3 feet (1 meter) from the soft bluffs each year. The rocks along the Pacific coast are harder and the cliffs taller. The tallest, most spectacular cliffs are made of strong rock like granite, formed when molten lava cooled. Shale, formed when dark clay is buried deep underground, is softer, and shale cliffs are much lower. Yet in time, the sea shatters even granite. At the base of those forbidding cliffs you can find rubble, rock that crashed to the sea as the water eroded the cliffs.

Erosion can be dramatic on a rocky coast. Over many years, waves gradually weaken a cliff, leaving it ready to collapse. Then a small earthquake, a severe storm, or the rumbling passage of a heavy truck can trigger a rockfall. Water lubricates rocks so they can slide easily over one another; thus heavy rains often cause landslides along cliffs. When heavy rains hit the West Coast, headlines tell of landslides that destroy homes or block the Pacific Coast Highway.

Northern California may be famous for its rugged coast, but southern California is known for its beaches. Most of the sand that built them came from the mountains that surround Los Angeles and San Diego. Periodic heavy rains washed the sand into rivers, which carried it from the mountains and dropped it along the coast. The beaches grew for thousands of years, but now they are shrinking. Southern Californians have dammed the rivers and paved their paths to the sea to prevent floods in the densely populated Los Angeles basin. Much of the sand is trapped behind the dams and never reaches the beaches.

River mouths are not the only places you find beaches along a rocky shore. Many beaches lie between two rocky points that stick out into the water. Once soft rock lay between the two points, but the ocean eroded it faster than the harder rock of the points. Now the waves pound hardest on the points. The sea and the rocks together shape each beach differently. Visit the several rocky beaches on Mount Desert Island in Maine, and you will see that each one is a little different.

River Deltas

The Los Angeles basin is made of dirt, sand, and rocks washed from the surrounding mountains during heavy storms. Those sediments do not have to go far to reach the ocean. Many other rivers carry sand and silt far downstream, then drop that load where the water slows down as it meets the sea. If it carries enough sediment, a river can form new land at its mouth, in a region called a "delta" because it is often triangular, like the Greek letter Δ (delta). This new land is flat and often marshy.

The largest river delta in the United States was formed in the Gulf of Mexico by the Mississippi River, sometimes called the "Big Muddy" because it carries so much silt. For thousands of years, it built the lowlands and marshes of southern Louisiana, adding about 1 to 2 square miles (2.5 to 5 square kilometers) a year of land until about 1900. Today, the Louisiana Delta, like Los Angeles beaches, is starved of sediment. With no new sediment added, the land is sinking as water oozes out of the muddy silt left by the river, and large areas of marsh are turning into open water.

Elevated and Submerged Coasts

What happens to old coasts when sea level changes? If sea level rises slowly enough, barrier islands can move with the oceans, but other coasts drown or are left high and dry. Geologists have found signs of these old coasts both above and below present water levels.

Although sea level has been rising for some eighteen thousand years, the land has been rising faster in a few areas. In southern California, earthquakes are pushing up some areas including the Palos Verdes Hills, the southwestern tip of the Los Angeles basin. Long ago, the hills were an offshore island, but today they are part of the mainland. A view from the side shows a series of thirteen terraces, each one a flat surface cut by waves, extending from a cliff toward the sea. Each of those levels was once the seacoast. In places along the East Coast, low ridges run roughly parallel to the shore; those ridges are the remains of ancient barrier islands formed between ice ages, when sea level was higher than today.

The oceans hide the evidence of coasts formed when water levels were lower. In some places, geologists can see clear signs of old coasts underwater, such as what appears to be a wave-cut coastline 330 feet (100 meters) underwater off the coast of British Columbia. Elsewhere, the waves have spread the sand from yesterday's beaches across the ocean bottom and put some of it on today's beaches.

Sea level rose rapidly for a few thousand years after the end of the Ice Age, but geologists believe sea level has risen only slightly the past few thousand years. That slow rise, about 1 foot (0.3 meter) every thousand years, let nature form stable shorelines around the world. Now, sea level is rising faster, threatening coasts around the world. Average sea level has been rising four to ten times faster in the last fifty to one hundred years—a rate that will increase as the world grows warmer. Before too long, today's coastlines may themselves be underwater.

4

Natural and Developed Coasts

The European explorers who sailed the North American shore looking for places to colonize were not impressed by the sites of today's coastal resorts. They considered sandy barrier islands bleak and unpromising for settlement. Most Native Americans felt the same way and used the islands only as fishing camps. Even the Dutch, who already had fought the sea for centuries, preferred dry land up the Hudson River to the sandy shore of Long Island.

Early European settlers did build seaports on the coast to maintain their ties across the Atlantic. Yet most ports, such as those in Boston, New York, Philadelphia, and Baltimore, were built on harbors protected from the open ocean. Pirates hid along some parts of the coast, and early settlers thought coastal land was almost worthless. In 1690, a Quaker colonist named Thomas Budd sold the present site of Atlantic City for four cents an acre, but sold inland property for ten times that price. About 1700, another settler sold the island that is now Wildwood, New Jersey, for nine pounds, to buy his wife a dress.

At the time of the American Revolution, most of the Atlantic shore was untouched except for seaports and fishing towns. Farmers wanted dry, fertile land where they could grow crops, not salty, marshy, or sandy soil. Well into the 1800s, many people thought that wetlands and lowlands were breeding grounds for disease. Early settlers left their opinions behind in names like "Dismal Swamp" near the Atlantic in Virginia and North Carolina.

The first coastal resorts date from the 1800s and were built near the larger cities of the time. Promoters advertised the benefits of sea air to residents of large cities. In the 1850s, the first trains ran from Philadelphia to Atlantic City and Cape May, New Jersey. The coast towns boomed, and hotels quickly replaced early boarding houses. Soon other railroads were built to the New Jersey shore, and more towns sprouted on other barrier islands. People came from New York, Philadelphia, and growing New Jersey cities like Newark, Camden, Trenton, and Paterson. Many liked the shore and built houses on the islands. As the island cities grew and more people had leisure time, the resorts grew as well. Today, except for a few parks, all 130 miles (209 kilometers) of the New Jersey shore is a long string of houses, condominiums, and resort development.

Other shore resorts also date from the 1800s. Development started in Nags Head, North Carolina, in the 1830s, and by the Civil War the town was a popular resort. Later, in 1903, the Wright brothers flew their first airplane just a few miles north of Nags Head. Because North Carolina is much farther from major cities than New Jersey, many of its barrier islands remain natural, including the Cape Hatteras and Cape Lookout national seashores.

In the late 1800s, new railroads opened the southern shore to development. People started building resorts in Florida in the early 1900s. Florida land prices soared in a land boom that ended after a 1926 hurricane devastated Miami and the Great Depression devastated the economy. However, another boom started after World War II and continues today.

Development Changes the Shore

One little cottage built in the dunes does little to change a barrier island. Suppose, however, more people come and build houses. Once enough people come, the state builds a road along the island and connects it to the mainland with a bridge. The road and the bridge bring still more people. Restaurants, shops, and boardwalks are built along the shore to serve them. Motels, hotels, and condominiums follow, and soon the sleepy island has become a resort town.

People change the face of any land where they build a town. Buildings and concrete and asphalt replace trees, wildflowers, and animals. A coastal resort is a city, dropped onto a long, low pile of sand beside the ocean. There is not much space on that pile of sand, so people build houses that they call "summer cottages" very close together or build condominium complexes that tower over the beach. Everyone wants to live close to the beach, because if you walk just a couple of blocks inland, the resort looks like any other city—except the ground is sandier, and the water may smell of salt spray if there aren't too many cars or trucks.

The people who build houses along the shore want to be near the ocean. Yet no matter how much they like the water, they do not want their houses full of sand or salt water. If the waves or the beach sand come too close, they will build walls or barriers to keep them out.

If you built a small shack to store your beach gear and fishing poles, you wouldn't spend much money to protect it from a heavy storm. However, you would spend more to protect a house on an expensive beachfront lot. The words "expensive" and "beachfront" go together these days. Land along the coast is so expensive that people measure its cost per foot of shoreline. Depending on the location, that price is $1,000 to $30,000. Usually, a lot must be at least 50 feet wide to hold a house, so the land alone would cost

$50,000 to $1.5 million—often much more than the house that is built on it.

Coastal land is so expensive that houses are crowded close together. The more the land costs, the more it pays to build big. If a lot costs a million dollars, few people can afford to build a home on it. However, if you build a twenty-unit condominium, you can divide the land cost among twenty people—reducing it to $50,000 each. Condominium developers like to say that they make the beach more accessible by building condos that more people can afford, but they aren't just being charitable. They also make more money that way.

The larger the buildings on the shore, the more money they cost. As the value of coastal property increases, it may seem reasonable to spend millions of dollars to defend that investment. The problem is that the defenses can destroy the old beach and stop nature from making a new one.

Natural Beaches and the Sea

We think of land as standing still. We move but the ground beneath our feet stays put. Natural ocean beaches are an exception to that rule. Wade in the tide, and the waves move the sand under your feet. As the tide rises, it washes away sand castles on the beach. Spend more than one day along the beach, and you can see day-to-day changes. A small stream may change its path to the water. Sandbars move toward the shore. A storm may reshape the beach, washing away sand that will later return on gentle waves. The water continually moves the sand.

The movement of the sand shapes the beach. So does the nature of the coast and the level of the sea. If the beach is trapped beneath a cliff or between rocky points sticking out into the water, it may have nowhere to go when sea level rises. The sand from the beach will end up underwater. However, if the land behind the shore is flat, the rising ocean pushes some sand inland in front of it, as high tide pushes strands of seaweed onto the beach. In this way, the sea can move natural barrier islands.

Geologists believe the barrier islands along the East Coast formed thousands of years ago, when sea level was much lower. Islands along the gently sloping North Carolina coast probably formed about fifteen thousand years ago 50 miles (80 kilometers) from to-day's shore. The rising sea pushed the shore, the sand, and the islands inland. The same thing happened when earlier ice ages ended; some barrier islands along the Georgia shore are built on islands left behind when sea level reached its peak during an earlier break between ice ages.

Ocean waves strike the outer beach of the barrier island, giving it the shape we saw in Figure 3–4. Storms and winds push some sand farther inland, creating a row of dunes, which is the highest point on the island. That high point isn't very high and in many places is no more than about 10 feet (3 meters) above sea level, but it is the backbone of the island. From there, the island slopes gradually down to the lagoon that separates it from the mainland. Usually grass and marsh divide the dunes from the lagoon. Sometimes it is hard to tell where the marshy back of the island "ends" and the lagoon begins. Some lagoons are so shallow that they are as much marsh as open water.

The beach normally absorbs energy from ocean waves. Storm waves lose most of their energy breaking on the dunes but push some sand back in an "overwash" zone. That extra sand helps build the back of the island. So do the remains of the grass and marsh plants. Plant roots also help stabilize a natural island.

The details differ from island to island, depending on sand sup-plies, local geology, and weather. Many islands are low and narrow; others are broad, and some have high dunes. Barrier islands along the North Carolina shore have large dunes 40 to 50 feet (12 to 15 meters) high, which move like dunes in the desert. Moving dunes on Currituck Banks and Bogue Banks have buried roads, trees, and

FIGURE 4–1: *In 1935, the Army Corps of Engineers built jetties to stabilize this inlet, which opened two years earlier between Ocean City, Maryland, and Assateague Island to the south. Since then, the rising sea has pushed undeveloped Assateague Island toward the mainland, while coastal defenses have kept developed Ocean City fixed. (Courtesy of Duke University Program for the Study of Developed Shorelines)*

homes. In the 1950s, a 75-foot (23-meter) dune called Penny's Hill started moving into the fishing village of Sea Gull, North Carolina. By 1964, most of the houses were covered. Today, some are reappearing, as are other houses on North Carolina barrier islands buried by dunes early in this century.

Other things can reappear, too. In 1626, a small ship named the *Sparrowhawk* sailed from Plymouth, England, carrying passengers and cargo bound for Jamestown, Virginia. It survived the Atlantic crossing only to become the first shipwreck recorded on Cape Cod, on the inner shore of the barrier island of Nauset Beach, a long spit that runs parallel to the Cape and acts like a barrier island connected at one end to the mainland. The waters off Cape Cod are treacherous, and many more wrecks followed. In 1863, shifting sands uncovered a wreck on the outer edge of Nauset Beach. Residents discovered it was the *Sparrowhawk*! In 237 years, the ocean had moved Nauset Beach over the wreck. Today, you can see the ship's remains in the Pilgrim Museum in Plymouth, Massachusetts.

Nauset Beach still moves. In 1889, the Coast and Geodetic Survey compared a new survey with one made twenty years earlier. They found that on the average, Nauset Beach had moved 8 feet (2.4 meters) inland over its entire 6-mile (10-kilometer) length. A recent survey shows that the movement continues.

Nauset Beach is not alone. All undeveloped barrier islands move inland as sea level rises. You can think of the island as "floating" on the edge of the sea, or being washed up like seaweed left behind at high tide. Different islands move at different speeds, some quite fast. The northern end of Assateague Island, along the Maryland coast, has moved completely off its original location since 1933, as shown in Figure 4–1. In many other places, the movement is only 3 to 6 feet (1 to 2 meters) a year.

How fast the beach moves depends on how fast sea level is rising. A small rise can produce a big change where the land slopes gently, as Figure 4–2 shows. If the land was perfectly smooth and rose 1 foot each 1,000 feet (or 1 meter each kilometer), a 1-inch (2.5-centimeter) rise would push the shore back 83 feet (25 meters). The shoreline does not retreat that fast because it is not perfectly smooth. It takes time for the ocean to push back the pile of sand that marks the shore, so the shore actually does not retreat that fast.

You can find evidence of this movement on natural beaches. In some places, old tree stumps and peat deposits poke out from under the sand. The trees and bogs never grew along the outer shore. Originally they were behind the dunes, on the back of the island, in the marsh or lagoon, or on the mainland. Rising sea level pushed the sand back over them until they emerged on the ocean side, like the remains of the *Sparrowhawk.*

You yourself may have collected evidence that barrier islands

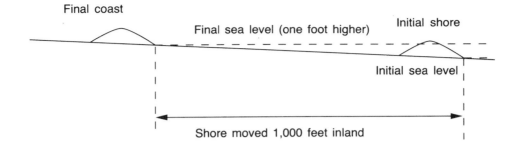

Final coast

Final sea level (one foot higher)　　Initial shore

Initial sea level

Shore moved 1,000 feet inland

FIGURE 4–2: *A small rise in sea level can push the sea far back onto flat land, here shown rising 1 foot every 1,000 feet from the sea (equal to 1 meter per kilometer). If sea level rises 1 inch (2.5 centimeters), the shore will retreat 83 feet (25 meters). The shoreline may not retreat this fast because the ocean takes time to move sand, but it does move many times faster than sea level rises.*

move. Most visitors to the seashore collect shells. Some shells come from ocean creatures and wash up with the tide. Others come from clams, oysters, and marsh snails, which normally live in the marsh or lagoon behind the island. How did they get to the beach? They didn't move—the beach came to them. The shells are fossils that were buried when the island moved over them. Some are thousands of years old.

When a barrier island moves slowly, it keeps about the same outline. The sandy beach remains in front, with dunes behind it, then lowlands and a shallow lagoon. On a natural island, the changes are not obvious because all the parts of the island move inland at about the same rate. If you visited the same island year after year, you might not notice the change, unless you checked a fixed landmark, such as a certain tree or a man-made property line.

Sometimes, sea level can rise faster than natural barrier islands can move, so the island shrinks on the inland side as well as on the beach. This can happen if the ocean does not wash new sand onto the back of the island, if the island's sand supply has been cut off, or if the local land is sinking, as it is along the Louisiana shore, where a few barrier islands may soon disappear.

Barrier islands are not all that moves as sea level rises. Behind the barriers, water rises in the lagoons, slowly flooding the coastal plain, turning dry land into marsh. The change is slow because marshes take time to form. If sea level rises slowly, new wetlands form about as fast as old wetlands turn into open water. If sea level rises too fast, wetlands can be lost because there is not enough time to form new marshes. Large areas of fresh-water marsh in Louisiana are turning into open water as rising salt water invades them and kills the fresh-water plants before salt-water plants can grow.

Inlets

The inlets that separate barrier islands from the mainland and from each other are not permanent. They change over the years as currents move the sand. New inlets form when the water breaks through weak spots, splitting an island in two or breaking a spit from the mainland to form an island. Strong ocean waves can push their way through a low spot in the dunes in a storm, pulling some sand into the ocean and pushing other sand into the lagoon. High water in the lagoon can break through the island, pushing its way into the ocean.

Sand dropped by ocean currents can clog old inlets. If the currents put more sand into the channel than they remove, it slowly becomes shallow, then fills in completely. Eventually, island sand will hide the place where the old inlet was. Inlets are most likely to clog if other inlets are nearby to let water flow between the ocean and the lagoon.

The opening and closing of inlets is natural. Old maps of the coast show many vanished inlets. New maps show different inlets. You can see these changes along the undeveloped shore, because people try to keep inlets from moving.

In some places, islands and inlets move in a natural cycle. Nauset Beach and Monomoy islands at the "elbow" of Cape Cod are one example. The maps in Figure 4–3 show the changes over many years. In colonial times, Nauset Beach extended across Chatham Harbor, protecting it from the ocean waves. In the early 1800s, Nauset Beach grew steadily south, as Monomoy retreated. In 1846, a storm cut through Nauset Beach in front of the harbor, exposing the mainland to strong ocean waves that caused erosion.

In the early 1900s, Nauset Beach grew south again, once again protecting Chatham Harbor as the inlet moved south. Eventually, it extended as far south as it had in the early 1800s. When the harbor was protected again, the shifting currents formed new land in the area that had eroded. In the 1930s, people built summer homes on the new land.

Nauset Beach became thinner as it grew southward, and in Janu-

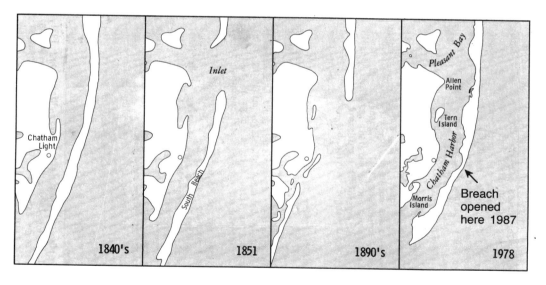

FIGURE 4–3: *Islands and sand spits at the southern tip of Cape Cod change in a cycle of about 140 years. In 1987, the ocean broke through Nauset Beach spit at the place shown by the arrow. (Courtesy of Stephen Leatherman, University of Maryland)*

ary 1987, a winter storm broke through it again, opening a new inlet. Since then, waves have widened the opening, once again exposing the mainland to the full force of ocean waves. The new land, deposited since the last time the inlet faced the harbor, began eroding. Little land was lost in summer 1987, but erosion was rapid in the fall and early winter. By January 1988, 75 feet (23 meters) of land was gone, and a house worth about $400,000 had collapsed into the water. Several other houses followed.

Developed Coasts

People who own property along the shore do not want to lose it to the rising ocean, but the change in sea level does not spare resorts, seaports, or other urban areas. When people protect their coastal property, they block the normal movement of the beach. They may think they can control erosion, but they are really turning the moving shore into a fixed rock sitting on the edge of the rising sea.

A sandy island starts turning into a rock when people draw property lines. They treat the ocean like any other troublesome neighbor and build walls to keep it "in its place" and off their land. The waves that try to push the beach sand inland are blocked by a seawall, the island's man-made armor against assault by the rising ocean. As the waves strike the seawall, they scour the sand from its base, and the beach starts to vanish.

If people live along the lagoon side of the island, they, too, start to worry about erosion. The natural processes that built up that land have been stopped, but the lagoon is rising along with the rest of the sea. Problems may be worse on the back of the island because it started out lower than the dunes facing the ocean. Many homes have been built on filled-in marshes just a few feet above sea level. Along the Florida coast, many heavily developed islands are armored on both the front and back.

Concrete seawalls fix the borders of heavily developed islands, turning them into giant concrete blocks resting along the shore. About seventy of the three hundred barrier islands lying along the Atlantic and Gulf coasts are "straitjacketed" by heavy development. They are not going anywhere. Their fate is up to the rising sea and human engineering skill, as we'll see in the next chapter.

5

Coastal Defenses

In 1888, the owners of the Brighton Beach Hotel on New York's Coney Island faced a problem. The hotel stood right on the sandy beach, and the sea was eroding the sand under it. Something had to be done quickly before the ocean undermined the building and destroyed it. The owners decided to jack the hotel up off the sand and put it onto freight cars that sat on parallel railroad tracks, as shown in Figure 5–1. Then locomotives pulled the cars—and the hotel— 617 feet (188 meters) to a safer location, where it stood until it was demolished in 1923.

For most of the past hundred years, owners of threatened buildings have taken a different approach. Instead of retreating from the sea, they have dumped rocks on the beach or built seawalls to blunt the force of the waves. The idea of armoring the coast is not new. The ancient Greeks and Romans built stone barriers to protect their harbors. The dikes that keep the North Sea from drowning Holland date back nearly a thousand years. In 1690, the Spanish settlers of St. Augustine, Florida, completed the first seawall in North America. But only in the last hundred years has coastal armoring become common.

Many coastal geologists believe that building "hard" defenses is the wrong choice. In the face of steadily rising sea level, they urge making a "strategic retreat" by moving buildings back from the shore as the Brighton Beach Hotel was moved a century ago. Small buildings are the easiest to move, but the National Park Service plans to move the 200-foot (61-meter) Cape Hatteras Lighthouse in North Carolina, threatened by erosion of Cape Hatteras Island.

However, retreat remains an exception. Some people consider it an admission of defeat. Others have no place to go because most coastal towns are divided into lots in the same way as other towns. If the sea erodes 3 feet (about 1 meter) a year from a lot 100-feet (30 meters) deep, the land will soon vanish. With or without a house, that lot is valuable, and the people who own it do not want to see their land—and their money—washed away. The owners want to defend it.

FIGURE 5–1: *Trains moved the Brighton Beach Hotel on Coney Island away from the Atlantic Ocean in 1888. The 617-foot (188-meter) move took a week. (From* Scientific American, *April 1888, Courtesy of Scientific American, Inc.)*

Coastal Defenses

Dunes on a barrier island are nature's defense against the ocean. The problem is that dunes migrate inland as the sea rises, but property lines are fixed. When the ocean starts knocking at their front door, owners of shorefront property turn to engineers for help. If they are not willing or able to move their houses, they have several alternatives. We will look at them in a rough order of their cost, effort, and impact on the coastal environment.

Some dunes cannot do their job because they have been damaged. People walking through the dunes, off-road vehicles, or construction can destroy the plants that stabilize dunes on many barrier islands. Once the plants are gone, the dunes can move, leaving houses behind them undefended or—even worse—blowing sand onto or into the houses.

Many coastal parks now fence off sandy dunes to keep people from walking through them. Others post signs asking people to walk on existing paths and stay off the plants. Some parks have laid temporary boardwalks—boards strung together by rope—on paths from parking lots to the beach. The goal is to protect fragile dune plants, whose roots help hold the dunes together.

Preserving the dunes is a good idea, but as sea level rises, natural dunes retreat inland. If people have built behind the dunes, they want the dunes to stay between their houses and the sea. Along much of the shore, people have built on top of the dunes, so they try to keep the dunes from moving. Rising sea level erodes the side of the dunes facing the ocean, but cannot push the dunes back.

Renewing the Beach

Most people think the beach is the most important part of the shore. When you go to visit a coastal resort, you spend time on the beach. If the beach starts to vanish, the resort is in trouble. What can be done when a broad beach shrinks? Many resorts have simply added new sand.

Engineers call the addition of sand "beach replenishment" or "beach nourishment." Sometimes they bring sand from the land on trucks, but usually they pump it in from offshore. A boat sits offshore and runs a hose down to the ocean bed. A pump that works like a vacuum cleaner sucks wet sand from underwater and pumps it through long, flexible hoses onto the shore. Engineers prefer to collect sand from places where there is too much, especially if it is blocking an inlet or boating channel.

The good news is that beach replenishment can recreate a broad, flat beach that vanished years ago. Figure 1–2 shows Miami Beach before and after beach replenishment. Before the sand was added, high tide came to the base of seawalls that kept "beachfront" hotels dry, and cynics joked about Miami "Beachless." Resort owners worried that they were losing their biggest tourist attraction. They were relieved when adding the sand gave visitors a beach again.

The bad news is that beach replenishment is expensive and won't last forever. Typically it costs $1 million to over $6 million per mile (1.6 kilometers) of beach—the bill for 10.5 miles (17 kilometers) of Miami Beach was $68 million in 1981. Sometimes the beach stays broad, but often the new sand vanishes faster than the old beach. Coastal engineers still find it hard to be sure how long the new sand will last. Miami Beach was lucky, and most of its 14 million cubic yards (11 million cubic meters) of new sand has stayed in place. However, Ocean City, New Jersey, saw 1.2 million cubic yards (1 million cubic meters) of sand, which cost $5.1 million, wash away in 2½ months. Most replenished beaches last longer, but in time all will need still more sand.

Other problems come because the new sand is not just like the old. Florida's beaches seem to have plenty of sand, but they receive little new sand. Most of the state's fine-grained old sand was washed from the north many years before or is made of ground-up shells.

Sand pumped from offshore may be coarser than the old, fine sand loved by tourists. It also can contain sharp, hard fragments of coral and limestone, which make a barefoot stroll along the beach un-pleasant.

Why does some new sand vanish much faster than the old beach? Engineers and geologists are not sure, which makes it hard to pre-dict how well beach replenishment will work. Sand texture may—or may not—be important. The new sand may be put in places where ocean currents are likely to remove it quickly. Some sand may be swallowed by the offshore hole from which it was pumped, just as high tide pushes the sand mountains you build on the beach back into the holes the sand came from.

Catching Sand

Ocean waves usually push sand and swimmers one way or the other along the shore. When you are in the water, you may not notice the little push from each wave, but when you come back to the beach you find you have moved away from your towel. The same current that moves you also moves sand up or down the beach. If rocks stick out into the water, they collect sand on the side that faces the current, but not on the other side.

Engineers use this fact to catch sand moving along a beach. They build a dam, or "groin," which sticks into the ocean as shown in Figure 5–2. The groin can be made of rocks, concrete, wood, steel, bags filled with sand, or even junked cars. It collects sand moving down the shore to build up the beach by the groin.

Groins do not solve the problem of rising sea level or cure a shortage of sand. The sand they collect would have built up beaches down the shore. Those beaches then start eroding faster, so people along them build their own groins. More groins are built, and soon groins line the beach, each greedily grasping for sand moving along

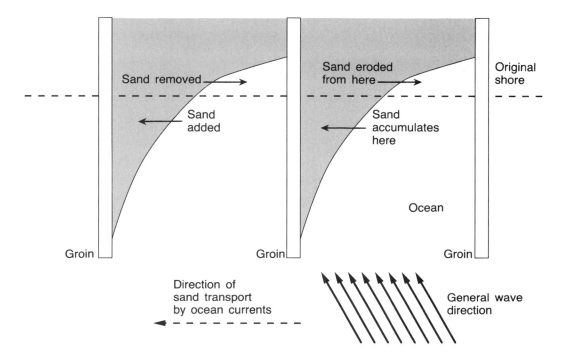

FIGURE 5–2: *Groins jut into the water to catch sand carried by currents running along the shore, but they speed erosion on the side of the groin away from the current.*

the shore. Groins don't solve any problems; they only control where the sand goes and fool some people into thinking they have "beat" erosion. Some groins seem so successful that people build houses or condominiums on the "new" beach, not realizing that the sea is still rising.

Other man-made barriers also stick out from the shore. Barriers called "jetties" stretch into the ocean at many inlets and river mouths, like the one shown in Figure 5–3. They are navigation aids, built to speed water flow and keep drifting sand from blocking the channel. Usually there are two jetties, one on each side of the flowing water.

Although their purpose is to keep shipping channels open, jetties

FIGURE 5–3: *Jetty at the east end of the Cape Cod Canal, with a lighthouse to direct mariners. Like many groins, this jetty is made of large blocks of rock.*

also act like groins and catch sand drifting along the shore. In many places, sand builds up along one jetty and erodes from the other. For example, a 1933 hurricane opened Ocean City Inlet in the barrier island just south of Ocean City, Maryland. In 1935, the U.S. Army Corps of Engineers built jetties to stabilize the inlet. Currents carry sand south in that region, so they built up sand along the northern jetty on the Ocean City side. To the south, Assateague Island was starved of sand and eroded rapidly, moving toward the mainland as shown in Figure 4–1.

Armoring the Coast

If someone throws things, you try to shield yourself. If the ocean throws waves at your house, you might put something in the way. Home owners and towns do that all along the shore. They start by putting rocks at the edge of the dunes or building a low bulkhead to keep water out of their yards. Once coastal engineering starts, it usually progresses to more and heavier armor. The ultimate defense is a massive stone and concrete seawall, like those defending many coastal cities.

Long ago, people discovered that an offshore sandbar weakened ocean waves. Strong waves would break over the sandbar, not smash into the shore. Sandbars do not stay in place, so engineers devised their own equivalent, called a "breakwater." The ancient Greeks built the first breakwaters of stone more than two thousand years ago to protect harbors. Today, engineers still use heavy rocks, often capped with concrete to help them withstand the pounding of ocean waves.

Breakwaters run parallel to the shore to create safe harbors for boats and to protect beaches. They are often used on the West Coast, where there are few natural harbors and deep ocean waves come close to the shore. Some breakwaters protect the harbor too well. One was built in 1933 to make a harbor for boats along the shore of Santa Monica, California. It calmed the waves so much that they stopped removing sand from the harbor, and in a year it became too shallow for boats. Meanwhile, beaches farther south shrank because Santa Monica Harbor had trapped the sand they needed.

Landowners usually prefer on-shore defenses. The simplest is dumping boulders on the beach, so they protect buildings behind them from ocean waves. That is what home owners in Chatham, Massachusetts, did in the winter of 1988 when the ocean started eroding the mainland rapidly. You can find many such piles in front of buildings along the shore, and a few are not made of rocks. At the height of a 1978 winter storm, the owner of a coastal home in La Jolla, California, called an engineering firm and asked for immediate help to protect his home. The engineers thought fast and sent workers to buy the cheapest used cars they could find. Then they parked the old cars on the beach in front of the man's house. When the storm was over, the cars were ready for the crusher, but the house had survived.

Rocks dumped on the edge of the beach are a stopgap. A better defense is to lay rocks, bags containing concrete, or concrete blocks carefully along the dunes, in a structure called a "revetment," shown in Figure 5–4. It does not need a poured concrete foundation and slants back from the water rather than standing straight up against the waves. Sitting at the top of the beach, revetments ab-sorb energy from storm waves that could erode the dunes behind them.

Another common defense is a low wall called a "bulkhead," shown in Figure 5–5. Usually built along the property line facing the ocean, a bulkhead may be wood, metal, plastic, stone, or con-crete. Wood bulkheads are common along the East Coast, with thick logs sunk deep into the sand, then bolted together on the top.

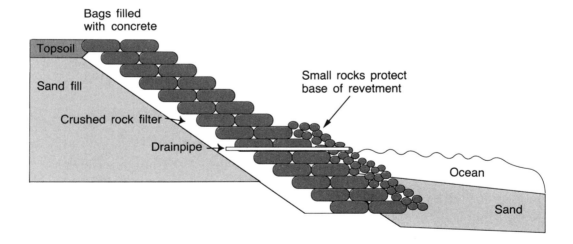

FIGURE 5–4: *A revetment slopes back from the beach. This one is made of bags containing cement, with rocks at its base to absorb some energy from ocean waves.*

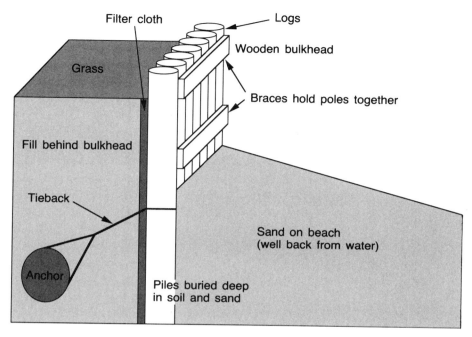

FIGURE 5–5: *A bulkhead made of wooden poles sunk into the sand at the top of a beach to keep strong waves from reaching the land behind it. Similar bulkheads are used as walls to line urban harbors but are not sunk in sand and have rocks at their base.*

On developed shores, bulkheads often mark the border between the public beach and private property.

Bulkheads can't survive the pounding of strong waves, but they can be put high on the beach, where storm waves reach them only once or twice a year. In places like Longport, New Jersey, a bulkhead at the end of the street marked the boundary between two worlds: the human world of houses, lawns, and streets, and the sandy world of the beach. Pavement and grass ran up to the town side of the bulkhead; sand ran up to the bulkhead on the beach side. Bulkheads also line urban harbors, where there are no strong waves, and they sit in the water like the wall of a swimming pool.

If looks were all that mattered, you might rather have a bulkhead than a revetment on your beach. A revetment covers part of the sand with rocks or concrete; a bulkhead looks like a small wall between the public beach and private property. However, a revetment is better for the beach. When waves break over smooth sand, they spread their energy over a large area. Their energy spreads over a smaller area on a sloping revetment, and they pound hard and head-on into a bulkhead or seawall.

You can feel the forces yourself if you stand in the water with your back to the waves. Stand straight up, and a strong wave hits very hard. Lean forward, like a revetment, and you feel less force as the waves run up your back. Waves bounce off a flat wall and scour sand away from the base of the wall; those that spread out on a flat surface remove little sand.

Revetments may do less damage than bulkheads, but they cannot preserve the beach forever. As sea level rises, the beach shrinks, and waves that break on the rocks take some sand away. Eventually, the waves are sure to top the structure, and the people who own land will demand a seawall.

A seawall is a massive fortification of concrete and stone. Stand at its base and you feel like a foot soldier outside a fort. The seawall rises 10 to 20 feet (3 to 6 meters) or more from the beach and is built massively to withstand the full power of mighty storms. The waves that bounce off the seawall steal the sand from its base. Stones and rubble sit at the base of the 21-foot (6.4-meter) seawall shown in Figure 5–6 that protects Galveston, Texas, from hurricanes roaring across the Gulf of Mexico. Little beach remains in front of the seawall at Monmouth Beach, New Jersey. Other coastal cities have sand in front of their seawalls only because the beach was replenished or the wall was built well back from the waterline.

Seawalls can protect coastal property, at least for a while, if you can sacrifice the beach and pay their stiff price—$300 to $1,000 per foot ($1,000 to $3,300 per meter) of shoreline. However, they take

FIGURE 5–6: *Stone and rubble protect the base of the Galveston seawall in this photograph from the 1920s. (Photo by W. T. Lee, Courtesy of U.S. Geological Survey)*

a constant beating from the waves and require regular maintenance. They can be undermined by the sea or by water seeping from the land. Seawalls have failed at Pacifica, California; Seabrook Island, South Carolina; South Padre Island, Texas; and elsewhere.

If sea level continues rising, many coastal cities will come to look like Holland, where massive dikes keep out the North Sea. The dikes are expensive to build and maintain, but the Dutch have little alternative; half of their land is below sea level, and they have no place else to go. Over the thousand years that the Dutch have battled the North Sea, floods have claimed thousands of lives. Millions of people live below sea level today in Holland, but few cities sit directly on the shore. Remarkably, the Dutch maintain beach resorts on barrier islands along their shore.

Damage from the Defense

Americans have not been as successful as the Dutch in preserving the coast they try to defend. Only one major city, New Orleans, lies below sea level, and it does not lie directly on the ocean. New Orleans never had an ocean beach; many of our armored coastal cities are losing theirs.

Coastal geologist Orrin H. Pilkey, Jr., of Duke University calls the problem "New Jerseyization." Old New Jersey resorts like Monmouth Beach and Sea Bright are horrible examples of beachless armored islands, where you must peer over the seawall to see the ocean. To be sure, you can find such islands outside of New Jersey, too. Some islands along the Florida coast may soon suffer the same fate, but they will be crowded with condominiums.

Coastal fortifications also speed the erosion of nearby, undeveloped beaches. They block supplies of sand that could build or maintain other beaches elsewhere. Groins and jetties capture sand that ocean currents otherwise would carry along the shore. The sand-starved beaches retreat quickly. An aerial photograph of Ocean City, Maryland, and Assateague Island to the south tells the story in Figure 4–1. The inlet between the two formed in 1933; the jetty built in 1935 blocked sand from reaching Assateague, and the starved island moved toward the mainland.

The public suffers because the undefended beaches are often public land. The National Park Service wants to keep the National Seashores natural, which means unfortified. Coastal armor typically protects private property—although public tax dollars may pay for its construction. Groins and other defenses also restrict public access to the beach.

In the long run, however, it is the natural beaches that will survive, because they can move inland with the rising sea. Susan Halsey of the New Jersey Marine Sciences Consortium predicts that the densely developed barrier islands along the New Jersey shore will be submerged as sea level rises. Anchored in place by roads and buildings, they cannot move. The armored islands are like rocks on the shore at low tide. As the tide rises, the ocean will cover them. History has proved again and again that even the mightiest fortifications cannot stand forever against a vastly stronger force such as the ocean.

6

Storms and the Coast

If you live along the southeastern coast of the United States, you know hurricane season. Each day in late summer and early fall, you watch the news and check the paper. You check maps that show tropical storms creeping across the Atlantic, and you get nervous if they head in your direction. Most of the dozen or so storms each year (not all hurricanes) miss you, but once in a while the National Hurricane Center in Miami will issue warnings for your area, and you will make preparations. People who live inland barricade the windows and bring everything inside, because strong storm winds can turn anything in their path into dangerous missiles. Those who live along the coast may have to evacuate their homes.

Powerful storms are facts of life on the coast. Hurricanes draw their power from the warm water and weaken once they reach land. The shore takes the hardest blows. A mighty hurricane that devastates the Texas coast is likely to be only a band of heavy rain when it crosses the Oklahoma border. Nature has shaped the coast to cope with storms, but people who build along the shore often forget that storms are part of nature.

68

FIGURE 6–1: *Houses along the coast of Mexico's Yucatan Peninsula, severely damaged by Hurricane Gilbert in 1988. (Courtesy of Robert Thieler IV, Duke University)*

Storms account for much coastal erosion, but you can't tell that from the usual "before" and "after" pictures, which show how only a stub of sand remains at a place where people relaxed on a beach in the 1890s. If you had watched the beach all the time between the two pictures, you would have seen both slow and fast changes. A heavy storm might push the beach back 5 feet (1.5 meters) in one day; then mild summer waves might return 4 feet (1.2 meters) of sand, leaving the beach only 1 foot (0.3 meter) narrower than before the storm. Currents along the shore shift from season to season, adding to the beach in summer and eroding it in winter.

Storms cause the most dramatic and dangerous changes. They build up tremendous energy over the ocean and bring heavy rains, high winds that drive huge waves against the beach and anything nearby, and a huge "storm surge" of water. A broad beach offers some protection from a big storm; a narrow beach gives little.

FIGURE 6–2: *Storm drives Atlantic Ocean onto Cape Hatteras Island. Cape Hatteras Lighthouse is in the background. (Photo by R. Dolan, Courtesy of U.S. Geological Survey)*

Storm-driven waves reach far above normal high tide to crash over bulkheads and seawalls and shatter houses that seemed safe in good weather. Figure 6–1 shows how Hurricane Gilbert destroyed homes on the Mexican coast in 1988. Figure 6–2 shows how a 1984 storm pushed water inland on Cape Hatteras Island on the North Carolina coast; Cape Hatteras Lighthouse is in the background. Television news shots don't show the worst of the storm; even the most daring camera crews know better than to walk out in the full fury of a hurricane.

Hurricanes

Hurricanes form when winds blow in a circle over warm ocean water in the summer or fall. They start as "tropical depressions," areas of low atmospheric pressure, with winds under 39 miles an hour (63 kilometers per hour). Often the winds pick up moisture and grow more powerful; if they reach 39 to 74 miles per hour (63 to 119 kilometers per hour), they become a "tropical storm." The growing storm forms an "eye," a central area where winds are mild and the weather comparatively clear. Just outside the eye, the storm is most intense. Atmospheric pressure continues to drop. If wind velocities pass 74 miles an hour (119 kilometers per hour), the storm becomes a hurricane. Hurricanes themselves also are classified by their severity, as shown in Table 6–1. The low pressure and storm intensity make the ocean rise up to 20 feet (6 meters) above normal sea level, in what is called a "storm surge." Similar storms occur elsewhere, but they have different names. They are called typhoons in the western Pacific, and cyclones in Australia and countries around the Indian Ocean.

Hurricanes are big, from 60 to over 900 miles (100 to 1,500 kilometers) in diameter. They bring heavy rains, and the strongest have winds that can exceed 150 miles an hour (240 kilometers per hour). The record for highest winds are not very accurate because the strongest storms blow away the weather instruments! The storm surge can devastate coastal cities.

TABLE 6–1: *Gradations of tropical storm*

Events or Scale No.	Central Pressures (millibars)	(inches)	Winds (mph)	Surge (feet)	Damage
Tropical depression	—	—	under 39	—	—
Tropical storm	—	—	39–74	—	—
Hurricanes					
1	over 979	over 28.91	75–95	4–5	minimal
2	965–979	28.48–28.91	96–110	6–8	moderate
3	945–964	27.90–28.47	111–130	9–12	extensive
4	920–944	27.17–27.89	131–155	13–18	extreme
5	under 920	under 27.17	over 155	over 18	catastrophic

Some storms drift harmlessly into the North Atlantic; others hit the mainland. Texas, Louisiana, and Florida are prime targets, but Atlantic hurricanes can hit anywhere from Central America to Massachusetts. Scientists watch hurricanes from satellites and airplanes, but they still find it hard to predict their paths more than a day or two in advance.

Hurricanes do not destroy everything in their path, but they can do tremendous damage. When a hurricane is coming, people evacuate the shore and low-lying barrier islands. Figure 6–3 shows what was left after a 1900 hurricane hit Galveston, Texas, without warning. The storm brings its heavy rains and high winds inland, but it is the battering wind-driven waves and storm surge that can nearly wipe barrier islands clean.

Many people survive hurricanes, but few feel the full force of the most intense part of a big storm. I was living in the Miami suburbs when Hurricane Donna passed through in 1960. The storm hit Flor-

FIGURE 6–3: *Galveston after a 1900 hurricane devastated the unprotected island. (Courtesy of Rosenberg Library, Galveston)*

ida from the south, devastating the Keys. We lived several miles inland, so we didn't have to evacuate, but we did block the windows with heavy cardboard and shut a heavy metal awning to protect the back of the house. The winds howled outside all night, and a part of a big tree came down on the house; but our lights never went out. The whole city was lucky; the center of the storm passed west of Miami, and the beachfront hotels suffered only modest damage.

Hurricane damage depends on a storm's strength, what part of it hits, and when and where it strikes. Many hurricanes weaken quickly as they pass over land and do less damage inland than some ordinary storms. Winds of 150 miles an hour (240 kilometers per hour) near the center of an intense hurricane are much more dangerous than winds of 75 miles an hour (120 kilometers per hour) farther out. Timing is important because flooding is much worse if the hurricane strikes at high tide than at low tide. The place the storm hits is important because some locations are much more vulnerable than others. If roads or canals cut straight across a barrier island, high water in the lagoon, pushed by strong winds, can follow their path to cut a new inlet to the ocean.

Nor'easters and Other Storms

People who have lived along the coast say that storms are worst in winter. The most severe storm I remember was not a hurricane but a winter storm New Englanders call a "nor'easter" because its winds come from the northeast. It hit the Boston area in February 1978, dropping up to 3 feet (almost 1 meter) of snow—although weather forecasts had called for only 6 inches (15 centimeters). Winds topped 120 miles per hour (193 kilometers per hour), well over the hurricane threshold. The Boston area was paralyzed, with thousands of cars stuck in highway snowdrifts. Snowplows couldn't cope with the mountains of white; it took a front-end loader to clear my street. Schools and businesses were closed for a week while people dug out. The damage was worst along the shore, where wind-driven waves knocked out Boston Edison's main power plant on Boston Harbor, destroyed homes, and damaged a seawall in Revere, Massachusetts.

Northeasters are the planet's largest and most powerful weather systems, but they do not get as much attention as their tropical cousins, hurricanes. Like hurricanes, their winds blow in circles, but they form over waters farther north and can sprawl across more than a thousand miles (1,600 kilometers). Unlike hurricanes, they can cross the entire United States. Their size and sometimes slow speed lets northeasters stay in one place for two or three days, battering the coast for much longer than a faster-moving hurricane. The Blizzard of 1978 pounded Boston for over two days; the most severe

FIGURE 6–4: *Effects of the "Ash Wednesday" storm of 1962 on coastal New Jersey. (Courtesy of Duke University Program for the Study of Developed Shorelines)*

coastal storm of the century, the "Ash Wednesday" storm of 1962, lasted for three days and caused extensive damage from Massachusetts to Florida. Figure 6–4 shows its effects on one part of the New Jersey coast.

Storms don't have to be severe to damage vulnerable or highly developed shore areas. A small northeaster on March 29, 1984, did about $160 million of damage to two highly developed towns on the New Jersey shore, Sea Bright and Monmouth Beach. Storms can speed erosion, cut new inlets in barrier islands, and deposit sand in places people don't want it. Later, calmer seas may return some of the sand, but they cannot rebuild a home or seawall.

Look carefully, and you can see changes from even small storms. After a heavy rain, little streams appear, cutting their own paths through the sand. Soon ocean waves and people's feet change the pattern, and the stream paths vanish.

Storm Frequency

Look at a weather map of the Atlantic in September, and you probably will see a hurricane or tropical storm somewhere. Each year, about a dozen storms get big enough to earn a name from the National Hurricane Center. Fortunately, the storms are too small to affect the entire coast and they do not hit the same place. A typical hurricane is a couple of hundred miles (320 kilometers) across, but North America has thousands of miles of seacoast where hurricanes can hit, from Massachusetts to Central America.

The chance of getting hit by a hurricane varies from place to place on the coast. The storms are most likely to strike southern and Gulf Coast states, but they can wander farther north. Key West, Florida, is a much more likely target than Providence, Rhode Island, but both were hit by severe storms in the 1930s. Hurricanes follow different paths, as shown in Figure 6–5, depending on weather at the time. Even such likely targets as Miami can go for many years between hurricanes.

The rarity of severe storms hitting any one place is both good and bad news. Nobody wants storm damage, but when storms are rare, people forget about the danger. A retired couple from Milwaukee may think the ocean is always as peaceful as on the summer day when they buy their beachfront condo. The real estate salesman from New York may believe so, too. People who live in an inland area brushed by a mild hurricane know nothing of the fury of a big storm hitting the coast. They are easily lulled into building too close to the shore.

We can look at storm threats by trying to imagine the worst possible in a certain period. Scientists and urban planners often talk about the "hundred-year storm"—the worst likely in a hundred years. In places like Miami, Charleston, or Galveston, that would be a direct hit by an intense storm like Hurricane Hugo, which hit Charleston in 1989. In Boston, the Blizzard of 1978 holds the title;

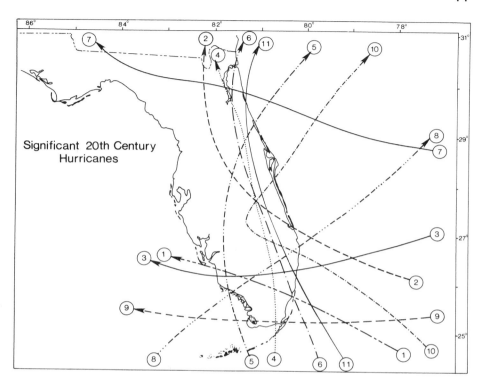

Significant 20th Century Hurricanes

1. September 1926
   ($112 million damage, 243 dead)
2. September 1928
   ($76 million damage, 1,836 dead)
3. September 1947
4. October 1950 (Hurricane King)
5. Donna, September 1960
   (went up East Coast, causing
   total of $426 million damage)

6. Cleo, August 1964
7. Dora, September 1964
8. Isabell, October 1964
9. Betsy, Aug.–Sept. 1965
10. Gerda, October 1969
11. David, Aug.–Sept. 1979

FIGURE 6–5: *Paths of some major Florida hurricanes. The 1935 storm is not shown because it did little damage to the Florida mainland, but it killed 405 people and did $46 million in damage to the Florida Keys. (Courtesy of Duke University Program for the Study of Developed Shorelines)*

in New York, it is the Blizzard of 1888. Such a storm can be much more severe than the worst storm likely in a ten-year period, as shown in Table 6–2. Surviving a hundred-year storm does not mean you can relax for another century. A similar storm could hit the next year—or wait two hundred years—because they come at random. The worst in so many years is only an average.

TABLE 6–2: *Differences in severity of storms likely at Atlantic City, New Jersey. The wave run-up tells how far above mean sea level the water will reach on the shore during a storm. It is even higher at some other parts of the New Jersey shore. Figures in parentheses are in meters.*

Type of storm	10-year	50-year	100-year
Chance of storm any year (%)	10	2	1
Storm surge (feet above mean sea level)	6.9 (2.1 m)	8.9 (2.7 m)	10.1 (3.1 m)
Wave height (feet)	5.6 (1.7 m)	9.1 (2.8 m)	10.6 (3.2 m)
Wave run-up (feet above mean sea level)	9.5 (2.9 m)	13.9 (4.2 m)	16.9 (5.2 m)

Weather records go far enough back in most of the United States for us to estimate the danger of a hundred-year storm. However, planning for a hundred-year storm cannot prevent all disasters, because more severe storms are possible. On February 1, 1953, the worst North Sea storm in modern times broke Dutch dikes in a hundred places and killed 1,835 people. Scientists believe such a storm can happen only once in eight hundred years. In response, Holland is spending billions of dollars on barriers to withstand the worst storm likely in four thousand years.

Storms and Disasters

Imagine living in a place where cars sometimes veer off the road and crash through your front yard and into your house. Life used to be like that for people living in "hurricane alley" on the East Coast. Sometimes they might get a warning from ships that skirted the storm, or islands hit by it, but a giant storm could strike without warning. Today, weather satellites and airplanes warn when trouble is coming—usually. However, unpleasant surprises still are possible. On October 16, 1987, the people of southern England were amazed to be hit by a small hurricane that destroyed thousands of trees and did much damage in a country not used to such storms. Winds of 93 miles an hour (149 kilometers per hour) were the strongest ever recorded at London's Heathrow Airport—nearly 31 miles an hour (50 kilometers per hour) above the previous record. Weather forecasters had seen the storm but thought it was much weaker.

The British storm was unusual; Europe rarely experiences hurricanes. Early settlers of the southeastern United States and the Caribbean islands learned about hurricanes the hard way. The first permanent European settlement in North America was St. Augustine, Florida, where by 1599 Spanish settlers had survived attacks by hostile Indians, British troops, and a hurricane. The city completed North America's first seawalls in 1690, but many years passed before settlers tried to conquer the swampy—and more hurricane-prone—reaches of southern Florida.

St. Augustine was not alone. A hurricane devastated New Orleans in 1722, four years after the city was founded. After another one struck in 1779, a newspaper reported that "all the vessels that were in the [Mississippi] river were either sunk or blown on shore; great numbers of houses in the town, though very low, were entirely blown down; and all the others suffered very considerably." The following year, another hurricane caused even more damage, but the survivors rebuilt the city. In 1856, a hurricane destroyed every building in Louisiana's first coastal resort on Isle Derniere, killing two hundred people. The resort had been one of the country's most attractive, but it was never rebuilt.

Arrival of a hurricane without warning often proved disastrous. The most deadly hurricane in United States history hit the un-prepared city of Galveston, Texas, on September 8, 1900. The city was a sitting duck. Nearly forty thousand people lived in the boom-ing town built on a barrier island along the Gulf of Mexico. Three miles across at its widest point, the island averaged only 4.5 feet (1.4 meters) above sea level. Rain and high winds arrived soon after dawn; by noon, both bridges to the mainland were flooded, blocking escape from the island. The storm grew stronger, destroying over twenty-six hundred homes, doing $25 million in damage, and covering much of the island with rubble, as shown in Figure 6–2. It killed six thousand people, injured another five thousand, and left ten thousand homeless.

Galveston residents did not give up. Within six days, they built a new bridge to the mainland. In 1902, the city began building a stone seawall, 3.3 miles (5.3 kilometers) long and 17 feet (5.2 meters) high, which helped the city survive a 1915 hurricane with only twelve casualties and $5 million in damage. Land level on the island was raised. Since then, the wall has been strengthened and extended to 10 miles (16 kilometers), but today little beach is left below the seawall. Galveston remains in danger; it was evacuated in 1988 when Hurricane Gilbert, one of the strongest hurricanes on record, roared through the Gulf of Mexico. Coastal geologists worry that rising sea level will make storm damage more likely in the future.

Many people who live along the shore know little about hur-ricanes, and that can get them into big trouble. Henry M. Flagler bought a large part of Miami Beach in 1882 and by 1896 had built the first railroad to Miami. Other developers followed, and land prices boomed as Northerners flocked south to enjoy warm winters. In 1900, only 1,681 people lived in Miami; by 1920, the number was over 100,000. Catastrophe arrived in September 1926 when a hurricane hit Miami with winds that reached 115 miles an hour (185 kilometers per hour) before blowing the instrument away. Storm tides reached 11.7 feet (3.6 meters). The calm eye of the storm lured many people outside, and most of the storm's 243 victims were trapped unprotected when the winds resumed. The storm caused $112 million in damage—close to $1 billion in today's money—destroyed 4,725 houses between Fort Lauderdale and Miami, and damaged 9,100 more. Two years later, another hurricane killed 1,836 people and did $76 million of damage in Florida. The Florida land boom was over.

Today's high-flying planes and weather satellites give early warnings of hurricanes, but they cannot stop property damage. Nor can they convince people to evacuate threatened areas. A few people always stay behind, some saying they want to protect their property or "experience" the storm, and others simply not willing to believe that a big storm will really hit.

People on the low-lying Gulf coast had plenty of warning before Camille, the most destructive hurricane to hit the United States in recent years, arrived in August 1969. Many left, but twenty-five residents of the new three-story Richelieu Apartments in Pass Christian, Mississippi, stayed behind for a hurricane party. They laughed as the police chief took down the names of their next of kin after they refused to leave. Only two survived—a ten-year-old boy and a woman who clung to part of her sofa as the ocean flooded her apartment. She spent ten uneasy hours riding the waves on her sofa, drifting out of sight of land before the next high tide washed her up on a beach 5 miles (8 kilometers) away. The other twenty-three were among the one hundred thirty killed by the storm's 25-foot (7.6-meter) surge. Damage was over $1 billion.

The storm that caused the worst erosion in the United States this century was not a hurricane but a northeaster, the Ash Wednesday storm of March 1962. Damage was severe because the storm came at the same time as the highest tides of the month. The high water wiped out coastal communities in Virginia and North Carolina, leveled islands in New Jersey and Massachusetts, and did extensive damage to Jacksonville, Florida. The grim statistics list $192 million in damage along the coast, about half in New Jersey, where floods damaged forty-five thousand homes.

Despite such records, the United States has been lucky—so far—with coastal storms. The most lethal storm was a cyclone that killed 300,000 people in Bangladesh on November 13, 1970. Many more died later of starvation. Arriving at high tide, the storm surge flooded 4,000 square miles (10,400 square kilometers) in the low-lying deltas of the Brahmaputra and Ganges rivers. Winds to 125 miles an hour (200 kilometers per hour) drove waves up to 50 feet (15 meters) high. The victims either did not hear or ignored warnings to evacuate the area.

Like Holland, Bangladesh is a small, densely populated country that lies close to sea level. However, Bangladesh is one of the world's poorest countries and cannot afford billions of dollars to protect against future storms. When the flood waters receded, new people moved onto the devastated land because it was open and fertile. The risk of future storms did not scare people worried about growing enough food to live from day to day.

Storm Legacies and Risks

Nature heals some storm damage. Calm seas bring back some sand that storm waves have swept off natural barrier islands. Natural islands may move inland, but they usually recover, although their landscapes may be changed, with new inlets opened and old ones closed.

The damage to people and property does not heal the same way.

If rebuilding is to be done, people must do it. Sometimes they are foolish and build on land swept clean by the last storm. Other people learn from their experience. Some move back from the shore or build more sturdily; others leave for safer ground away from the coast.

Those of us who have survived storms remember them. One of the nation's leading coastal geologists, Orrin H. Pilkey, Jr., of Duke University, traces his interest in the coast partly to his retired parents' encounter with Hurricane Camille in 1969. Before the storm, Pilkey's father had pointed out examples of good and bad construction in Waveland, Mississippi, but even the good work, if it was too close to the ocean, did not survive Camille. Two rows of houses had stood between the Pilkeys' house and the ocean; the hurricane had reduced the first row to rubble and partly destroyed the second. The Pilkeys' house survived, but the family decided to move to Virginia after shoveling out the mud.

New people are always coming to the southern shore. You may hear your grandparents talking wistfully about "moving south," especially when the weather is bad in winter. Tired of snow and ice, they want to live where it is warm in January. Some retired people do move south, buying shorefront condos and relaxing on the beach. It can be a pleasant life when the weather is good, but people like Pilkey worry about what might happen if a hurricane strikes a barrier island built high with retirement condos. Linked by only a few bridges to the mainland, such islands are hard to evacuate at the best of times. It gets much harder if high-rise buildings are filled with thousands of elderly people, some of whom are frail, slow moving, or handicapped.

7

Vanishing Places

The map of Cape Cod National Seashore shows Marconi Station on the Atlantic coast in Wellfleet. In 1901, radio pioneer Guglielmo Marconi built four giant towers overlooking the ocean to send "wireless" signals across the Atlantic. During World War I, the towers were torn down. Today, all that remains are a few plaques and the base of one tower. Erosion has claimed the sites of the other towers. Before long, the last one will vanish; each year the ocean removes an average of 2 to 3 feet (0.6 to 1 meter) from the outer edge of the sandy cliff.

The Marconi Station site is one of many places that is changing as our shores shift. Farther north on Cape Cod, erosion threatens Highland Light in Truro. For well over a hundred years, the oceans have swallowed lighthouses built too close to the water from Maine to Alaska. Yet except for a few historic sites like Marconi Station, you won't find markers to tell what has vanished from the shore.

Local old-timers might remember when the beach was broader or when a big storm destroyed an old hotel that stood by the water. Old maps in the local library may show a shoreline different from the one in modern maps. Compare old and new maps carefully, and you may find that a street along the edge of an ocean cliff has vanished. Land is not all that has vanished. In many urban areas, people have filled in wetlands and shallow bays and built upon them. Much of Boston was once a shallow bay. Since 1850, landfill and silting have shrank San Francisco Bay by over 40 percent to its present 400 square miles (1,000 square kilometers).

The Drowning of Dunwich

America is young compared to Europe, where history goes back thousands of years. One of the world's oldest and most intriguing of legends is of Atlantis, a great civilization that supposedly sank under the sea in a single great catastrophe. Despite many claims, no one has found Atlantis underwater, but people have found remains of other drowned cities. They lay not in the ocean depths, but in the shallow water just offshore. They are coastal cities that sank underwater as sea level rose.

The Atlantis legend comes from Greece, a land of earthquakes and volcanoes, which can make the land rise and fall. In northern Europe, it is the North Sea that is rising, threatening gently sloping shores in England, Holland, France, Belgium, Germany, and Denmark. Old records show how the steady rise of the North Sea has claimed some coastal towns. One was Dunwich, which became an important port and farming center after the Normans conquered England in 1066. Troubles began within a few hundred years. A 1328 storm filled the harbor with sand and silt, and the sea began its steady march into the town. In the 1500s, the North Sea claimed the church of St. John Baptist and three chapels. In the 1600s, it surrounded the town hall. In 1715, it drowned the jail. In 1740, strong winds destroyed the cliffs, the last remains of the churches, and most of the rest of the city. In the nineteenth century, a new Dunwich was built.

Archaeologists suspect that the oceans may hide some early remains of human habitation in North America. Sea level was much lower when the first people reached North America during the Ice Age and for thousands of years afterward. Many early North Americans may have lived near the shores of the time in areas long since covered by the rising seas. Canadian geologists recently discovered that the continental shelf off British Columbia was above sea level ten thousand years ago. That land was rolling hills and would have been much easier for people to travel than today's rugged Canadian western coast, so they suspect that people lived there.

"New Jerseyization"

In historic times, North America has lost a handful of tiny shoreline towns, often abandoned after devastating storms. Subtle changes are more common. Many older coastal resorts have lost their beaches, by the process Professor Orrin H. Pilkey, Jr., calls "New Jerseyization." Anyone who has visited the New Jersey shore will understand why. Most of the 130 miles (200 kilometers) of shoreline are packed tightly with houses. In the late 1970s, less than two hundred vacant oceanfront lots remained along the entire privately owned shore. As rising sea level tried to push the shoreline inland, owners of coastal land built bigger defenses. Today, huge seawalls protect resorts that have little or no beach left above the high-tide mark.

New Jersey's misfortune was to be too close to big cities. In 1801, a Philadelphia newspaper ran the country's first advertisement to attract people to a beach. Ellis Hughes, then postmaster of Cape May, called the town at the southern tip of New Jersey "the most delightful spot that citizens can go in the hot season." By the Civil War, Cape May was the country's most prestigious beach resort. Six presidents vacationed there during the 1800s. In 1908, Henry Ford raced his newest cars on the city's beaches.

Today, Cape May does not have enough beaches for car races. The city is almost broke. Trying to get a federal grant to build

FIGURE 7–1: *A rubble seawall at Cape May, where the beach has vanished. (Courtesy of Duke University Program for the Study of Developed Shorelines)*

groins, city officials wrote, "Maps show that blocks have been lost, that a boardwalk has been lost. . . . The stone wall, one mile long, that we erected along the ocean front only five years ago has already begun to crumble from the pounding of the waves since there is little or no beach. . . . We have finally reached a point where we no longer have beaches to erode." You can see that in Figure 7–1.

The sad story of Cape May repeats itself up and down the New Jersey shore. The state's best-known coastal resort, Atlantic City, was born in 1854 when a railroad was built from Philadelphia. The first boardwalk came in 1870, and other more famous ones have followed since. By the turn of the century, houses had reached the south tip of the island at Longport, which washed away a few years later.

After the 1950s, Atlantic City began sliding into seediness and slums. Most of the beach sand was gone. High tides during the 1962 Ash Wednesday storm flooded most of the island, and in some places water was 5 feet (1.5 meters) deep. Since then, the state has replenished the beach with new sand, and Atlantic City still considers itself a coastal resort. However, its main attraction is casino gambling, legalized in the 1970s.

New Jerseyization is not limited to New Jersey. One sunny summer day, I drove my family to Marshfield, Massachusetts, searching for a beach shown on the map. The beach was there, at the base of a huge seawall that ran along the road. The cottages on the other side were packed together like on a city street. To get to the beach, we climbed a few steps to the top of the seawall, which was a few feet above the street. A long set of concrete steps on the other side took us to the strip of sand 10 to 15 feet (3 to 4.6 meters) below street level. The beach seemed wide at low tide, but it shrank as the tide rose. Groins jutted out from the shore, but they had not saved the beach.

You can find seawalls all along the coast. Many people take them for granted, because they are part of the only seacoast they have known. Others accept them as part of the price of living along the shore. If you know natural beaches, however, seawall shores seem about as natural as swimming pools. Viewed from the ocean or the beach, as in Figure 7–2, a seawall is as formidable and forbidding as the walls of a fort.

Condomania

The popular writer John MacDonald picked Florida as the site for his best-selling thriller *Condominium*, which later was made into a movie. It was a good choice; Florida's shores are packed with condos. In MacDonald's story, a shady developer builds high-rise condos on a vulnerable island, without a proper foundation. A heroic engineer warns that a storm could turn the building site into a new

FIGURE 7–2: *Viewed from the ocean, this seawall in Harpswell, Maine, looks like a fortification. (Courtesy of Army Corps of Engineers)*

inlet, and a hurricane soon arrives, demolishing the building and killing people foolish enough to have ignored the storm alert.

Fortunately, most big buildings along the shore are constructed properly. However, the bigger they are, the larger the investment and the more pressure to build seawalls to protect them. Many condos are built with seawalls sculpted into the landscape, as if they belonged. Beaches still remain in front of most buildings, but coastal geologists expect it will only be a matter of time before the beaches start to vanish. Strange as it may seem, sand is in short supply on the Florida shore, because rivers and ocean currents are not bringing much new sand. If we lose today's sand, it will be hard to replace.

Some people call the spread of beachfront condos "Floridaization," but it is not limited to Florida. I found condos sprouting on

FIGURE 7–3: *Condominium being built along the beach in Old Orchard Beach, Maine. The dark material on the beach is seaweed left by a high tide.*

the edge of the beach in Old Orchard Beach, Maine, when I visited there in 1988, as shown in Figure 7–3. You can find them in New Jersey, the Carolinas, and most other coastal states as well.

Lighthouses

Because they have always been built close to the coast, lighthouses may be the best markers to gauge the shifting of the shore. Their bright lights steadily scanned the surrounding sea, warning sailors from dangerous waters where rocks and sand shoals might destroy their ships. Over the years, many have fallen into the sea, sometimes taking lighthouse keepers with them. Others have survived because they were set back from the water's edge.

In 1797, the United States built Montauk Point Light at the east end of Long Island. President George Washington, himself an engineer and surveyor, had the lighthouse built 200 feet (61 meters) from the sea and predicted it would stand for two hundred years. Today, less than 40 feet (12 meters) of land remains between Montauk Point Light and the cliff's edge.

The stormy, shallow waters of the North Carolina coast are among the most dangerous along the entire North American coast. The most southern of the three points jutting out from barrier islands on North Carolina's shore is named Cape Fear. The "Diamond Shoals" off the northern point, Cape Hatteras, have wrecked at least six hundred ships, earning them the name the "Graveyard of the Atlantic." To warn away boats, the Coast Guard in 1870 built on Cape Hatteras the tallest brick lighthouse in the United States.

In 1870, the 200-foot (61-meter) lighthouse on Hatteras Island stood 1,500 feet (460 meters) from the Atlantic. By 1935, sixty-five years later, erosion had cut the shore back 1,400 feet (430 meters), so the lighthouse was only 100 feet (30 meters) from the water. In the 1930s, groins were installed to protect the lighthouse, and the Civilian Conservation Corps built sand dunes along the entire island. Sand was pumped onto the beach and a revetment was built of sandbags in the 1960s.

Those efforts may have delayed the lighthouse's doom, but they did not end the danger. The beach near the lighthouse projects into the water and is unusually steep. A panel of the National Academy of Sciences warned in 1988 that a severe storm could destroy the lighthouse. A seawall might save it for a while, but the panel worried that construction might damage the lighthouse, and that even a seawall might be vulnerable. Instead, the panel recommended moving the lighthouse, and the National Park Service decided to move it about 2,300 feet (700 meters) southwest. That should protect the lighthouse from erosion for another hundred years.

Cape Cod

People who live in New England often call Cape Cod old, but geo-logically it is young. Cape Cod is made of deposits left by glaciers that melted fifteen thousand to eighteen thousand years ago. Nan-tucket and Martha's Vineyard, islands to its south, and New York's Long Island were formed in the same way. When the ice melted, Cape Cod and the islands were hills on a coastal plain. The rising oceans gave them their present shape, and the stormy Atlantic con-tinues to reshape Cape Cod. It pounds on the outer arm of the Cape, pushing sand north and south and eroding the cliffs overlook-ing the ocean 1 to 8 feet (0.3 to 2.4 meters) a year. Left to itself, in a few thousand years the ocean will break through Cape Cod, leav-ing the north tip of the outer arm as an island.

Until this century, most people did not care much. The Pilgrims made their first landing on Cape Cod, but didn't like the sandy peninsula and sailed on to settle in Plymouth. In the 1700s and 1800s, Cape Cod was home to fishermen and whalers, but it was poor farmland even compared to the rest of rocky New England. Now, like other sandy shores near big cities, it has become a popu-lar, and sometimes crowded, summer resort.

The stuff of Cape Cod is not hard rock but soft soil, sand, and boulders. Walk along the outside of the Cape's outer arm—the up-raised upper arm facing the Atlantic—and you look up at sand-laden cliffs, 60 to 170 feet (18 to 52 meters) tall. Once the land sloped more smoothly to the sea, like the side of the Cape facing the mainland. However, for thousands of years the ocean has dug into the cliffs, changing the shape of the Cape, as shown in Figure 7–4.

The sand the ocean takes from the bluffs does not vanish. Ocean currents push it both north and south along the shore, forming sandy beaches. Provincetown, at the northern tip of Cape Cod, is

FIGURE 7–4: *When the rising Atlantic reached Cape Cod about 3,500 years ago, its upper arm was uneven, as shown by the solid line. Over thousands of years, the Atlantic Ocean has smoothed out its shores, taking sand from the bluffs to build land to the north and south, forming the present coast, shown by the dotted line. (From A Geologist's View of Cape Cod, by Arthur N. Strachler, Copyright 1966 by Arthur N. Strachler. Reprinted by permission of Doubleday, a division of Bantam, Doubleday, Dell Publishing Group, Inc.)*

built on that sand. The sand that washes south forms barrier islands along the shore.

Most of the outer edge of Cape Cod is part of Cape Cod National Seashore. The National Park Service tries to limit damage to the bluffs by controlling where people walk, but it recognizes that nature is eroding the cliffs. The National Park Service will not build seawalls. If buildings along the cliffs are threatened, it will move them inland or let them fall into the sea.

The National Park Service has the same policy for all its national seashores, including Assateague Island National Seashore in Maryland, Cape Hatteras National Seashore off the North Carolina coast, Cumberland Island National Seashore in Georgia, Canaveral National Seashore in Florida, Fire Island National Seashore along the southern edge of Long Island, Padre Island National Seashore in Texas, and Point Reyes National Seashore in California. Except for

Cape Cod and Point Reyes, all the national seashores are barrier islands that will migrate inland as sea level rises.

As the ocean changes these lands, it may uncover more long-lost relics like the wreck of the *Sparrowhawk*. Hundreds of years ago, pirates roamed the East Coast and sheltered in areas remote from ports of the time. Most of them spent their ill-gotten gains as fast as they could steal them. Some became rich enough to buy pardons from kings. But a few treasures are missing, like the hoard of Captain William Kidd, who was hanged in London in 1701. Could some of those treasures be buried in areas that are now eroding? We don't know, but it is possible that someday, somewhere, ocean waves might dig out a long-forgotten treasure and spill it onto the shore.

Landslides and Land Loss

The scenery is spectacular along the Pacific Coast Highway for 30 miles (50 kilometers) west of Santa Monica. The trip takes you through towns like Malibu and past beaches at the base of the Santa Monica Mountains. Expensive houses perch at the top of the hills and huddle near the shoreline. Once in a while, the hills come crashing down to the sea.

Landslides are part of life along the Pacific Coast Highway, which runs the length of California. The road wanders along the shore, sometimes near the water, sometimes along the edge of the cliffs above. Much of the rock is soft. Heavy rains or the attack of the ocean can weaken the rock further, until it is too weak to support the steep cliff. Then, with little or no warning, the rocks and mud tumble down onto the highway, the beach, or onto beach houses foolishly built along the base of the cliffs.

Figure 7–5 shows a 1958 landslide in Pacific Palisades, which dumped many tons of dirt and rock onto the Pacific Coast Highway. It blocked the road and spilled over the beach. Geologist K. O.

FIGURE 7–5: *1958 landslide blocks the Pacific Coast Highway in Pacific Palisades, California. (Photo by J. T. McGill, Courtesy of U.S. Geological Survey)*

Emery once counted twenty-one landslides in 5 miles (8 kilometers) along the Santa Monica Mountains. If you ride along the Pacific Coast Highway, don't be surprised to see barriers warning you away from the edge of the road—either because rocks have fallen onto the road from above or because part of the road has slipped toward the ocean.

As the cliffs slide into the ocean, land vanishes. Century-old maps of Encinitas, a town north of San Diego, show Sixth Street closest to the ocean cliffs. Today, the cliff houses are on Fourth Street. Nobody remembers Sixth Street, and Fifth Street was closed in 1946. Geologist Gerry Kuhn found that the cliffs in Encinitas have retreated up to 800 feet (240 meters) since 1880—about half of that after severe floods between 1883 and 1889. He also found a fascinating pattern in the town's tax records. A coastal building lot initially had a high value, but that value started dropping as the land fell into the Pacific. Eventually, the property value vanished along with the land—but the value of the next lot inland rose, as it became the land closest to the sea.

Erosion and landslides occur all along the California coast at different rates, but like earthquakes, they don't seem to bother the natives. Some houses perch near the edge of the cliffs, like the one in Figure 3–5, and a few dangle over the edge, spectacularly supported by beams braced against the rocks. Often the more dangerous the dwelling, the higher the price.

Land loss is not unique to California. In 1987, three geologists from the Woods Hole Oceanographic Institution calculated that Massachusetts was losing 60 acres of land a year to rising sea level. Coastal wetlands are the most vulnerable areas because they generally lie within about 3 feet (1 meter) of sea level. A study by the Environmental Protection Agency (EPA) warns that the continuing sea-level rise could destroy large areas of coastal wetlands. Even counting the natural addition of sediment to marshes, the EPA study says that the United States could lose 47 percent to 81 percent of its coastal wetlands to rising sea level by 2100.

8

Lake and River Shores

Changes in the ocean shore may seem remote if you live in Chicago, Cleveland, St. Louis, or Salt Lake City. Those cities have shores, but they lie along lakes or rivers. Those shores are quite different from ocean shores, but they, too, can change.

Lakes and rivers can rise much faster than sea level. Rivers change fastest because water flows through them. Like a faucet, a river stops flowing if you turn the water off, although usually only desert rivers dry up completely. Rivers can flood in a few weeks in the spring, as snows melt and heavy spring rains fall, adding water until the rivers spill over their banks. That flooding is part of a natural seasonal cycle, in which river levels rise and fall. Flood levels vary from year to year, so a place that was dry when people picked it as a town site may be flooded a few years later.

A few rivers flow into landlocked lakes like Great Salt Lake in Utah, but most flow to the sea. There they shape the shore. River water carries sand and silt, which it drops as it slows down at the river mouth. The sediments build up the land at the mouth of the river, so it grows into the sea. The sand also nourishes beaches up and down the shore.

Lake levels change, too. From 1964 to 1986, Great Salt Lake in Utah rose 20 feet (6 meters). That's a big change for a shallow lake that normally covers 1,361 square miles (3,500 square kilometers). In 1964, the lake was at the lowest level since records began in 1847—no more than 17 feet (5 meters) deep—and some people worried that it might dry up. In 1986, it topped the highest level on record, flooding 770 square miles (2,000 square kilometers) and causing over $200 million in damage. To control lake level, the desperate state of Utah pumped water into nearby low desert areas.

Differences from the Seashore

The differences between lake and river shores and ocean shores arise from the differences between the bodies of water. Waves grow as winds blow over water; the longer the distance and the stronger the winds, the bigger the waves. Waves that reach the seacoast may have started thousands of miles away. The Great Lakes are much smaller, so their waves are usually smaller than those reaching most beaches facing the open ocean, although winter storms create large waves at some places on the Great Lakes. Smaller lakes usually have only tiny waves, although strong winds can stir up waves a couple of feet (half a meter) high on a lake 5 miles (8 kilometers) across. The same winds would make much larger waves in the ocean.

The size of the oceans also gives them large tides, typically 3 feet (1 meter) or more. Most lake tides are too small to measure; the biggest in the Great Lakes are only 1.7 inches (4.3 centimeters).

The steady pounding of waves, the rising and falling of the tides, and the mighty waves of strong ocean storms combine to form broad ocean beaches. Lake and river shores do not suffer the same punishment that shatters rocks into sand and spreads it about the beach. Some places have sandy beaches, but in many places trees and grass grow right to the waterline, especially on rivers and small lakes. Trees and grass grow close to the ocean only in protected inlets and bays where strong waves are rare. A surprising number of lake beaches are artificial, made of sand brought by people who live along the shore.

Another difference is the water. Except for Great Salt Lake, the Caspian Sea, and a handful of others around the world, lakes and rivers are fresh water. The oceans are salt water. Few land plants and animals can survive exposure to salt water; you and your lawn would die if you had only salt water to drink. Some plants can tolerate the salt spray tossed into the air by the ocean, but almost none can survive the constant beating of ocean waves on an ocean beach. Salt water helps create the open beach and reserves the shore zone for plants and animals that can tolerate it.

Rivers and lakes rise and fall more slowly than ocean tides, but they may change over a larger range. In the summer, grass and weeds grow in the dry outer edges of riverbeds. In the spring, high water will sweep the riverbed clean, so the grass and weeds can start again once the water level falls. Trees cannot survive that annual rise and fall of the river, so they grow only where flooding is rare.

Some trees beside rivers and lakes tilt over the water, as if they are ready to fall in, as shown in Figure 8–1. Eventually many of them will. They lean toward the water because waves or rising water level have washed away the dirt under their roots. Rising lakes undermine some trees, but more often the cause is the waves that trail out like a V behind boats. The faster the boat and the more powerful the motor, the bigger the waves. Sit beside a quiet lake or river, and you can see that boats make the biggest waves. Those waves erode the shore, even when the boats stay clear. The more boats and the faster they travel, the more erosion.

The Mississippi—the Father of Waters

The Chippewa Indians called the Mississippi River the "father of waters." It is a good name for a mighty river that collects water from

FIGURE 8–1: *Trees tilt over the Songo River in Maine. The wakes of passing boats undermined the roots on the riverbank, causing them to tip toward the water.*

the Rocky Mountains to the Alleghenies. The Mississippi drains over a million square miles (3 million square kilometers) of the United States—41 percent of the land area of the forty-eight states (excluding Alaska and Hawaii). The only river in the world that collects water from a larger area is the Amazon in South America. The Mississippi's path is ancient; for millions of years, water from central North America has flowed south into the Gulf of Mexico.

Like all rivers, the Mississippi carries sand and silt that the rains have washed from the land upstream. People call the river the "Big Muddy" because it carries so much sand and silt—hundreds of millions of tons a year. The water drops some sediment as it flows slowly across the plains and drops the rest when it reaches the sea. Over millions of years, the Mississippi and its ancestors have deposited sediment 3 miles (5 kilometers) thick along the present Gulf coast.

The river is highest and muddiest in the spring, when it carries water from melting snow. For thousands of years, the river spilled over its banks each spring, depositing rich silt on low-lying "flood plains." People settled along the river to farm the fertile flood plains, but they did not want the floods. Starting in the 1700s, they built dikes, or "levees," to keep the river in its banks. Levees line the shores of river cities like New Orleans and St. Louis. Since the late 1800s, the Army Corps of Engineers has built and maintained levees along most of the lower Mississippi.

Where the land is almost flat, near its mouth, the river builds its own "natural" levees. It drops some sediment each time it flows over its banks, and the piles grow biggest closest to the river. Slowly, the natural levees build up above the rest of the land. Meanwhile, some sand and silt fall on the riverbed, raising its level. Eventually, the riverbed can become higher than the surrounding land, as shown in Figure 8–2.

A natural river drops most of its sediment load at its mouth, where the water slows as it meets the sea. Over many years, the sediments build up a flat delta, at the river mouth, and the river splits into many separate streams that wind across the flat area to the sea. The Mississippi River Delta covers most of southern Louisiana.

People found the silt dumped by the Mississippi as much of a problem as floods. The steamboats that started running up and down the river in the 1800s could get stuck if too much sediment built up on the river bottom. By the late 1800s, the Army Corps of Engineers was dredging a channel so boats could travel the Mississippi.

The Mississippi follows a winding course, which you can see most easily as the western boundary of the state of Mississippi. The river "meanders" so much because it flows slowly through the flat area, dropping sediment that clogs its path. In time, the channel becomes so shallow that the river finds another course. The curves make the river much longer than if it were straight, so the Army Corps of

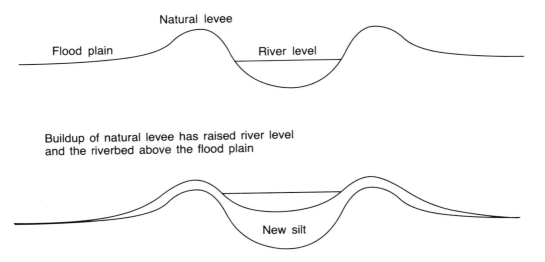

River with natural levee in flood plain

Natural levee

Flood plain   River level

Buildup of natural levee has raised river level
and the riverbed above the flood plain

New silt

FIGURE 8–2: *Silt deposited by a slow-flowing river builds natural levees along the river edge and fills in the river bottom until it can be higher than the surrounding land. Such natural levees are high points in the Mississippi River Delta near the Louisiana coast.*

Engineers cut through some curves to shorten the river's path, hoping to speed travel and improve water flow.

The Shrinking Delta

Growth of a river delta depends on a delicate balancing act. New sediment and growth of the marsh add to the height of the land. However, new sediments squeeze out the water that is 80 percent of the river mud, so the land underneath sinks. The weight of the new sediment also pushes down the continent beneath. Meanwhile, worldwide sea level is rising. For the delta to grow, the land must rise faster than the water.

Dams and channels on the river started affecting the Mississippi

Delta about 1900. Until then, river sediments formed 1 to 2 square miles (2.5 to 5 square kilometers) of new land a year. Since then, the sediment that had helped build new land has been caught by dams upstream, or flushed through the river channel and dumped into deep water beyond the river mouth. Without that new sediment the delta is shrinking. Each year, about 40 square miles (100 square kilometers) of Louisiana marsh turn into open water. Much of the loss occurs 5 to 10 miles (8 to 16 kilometers) inland, where salt water kills plants in fresh-water marshes. Louisiana has nearly half the coastal wetlands in the lower forty-eight states, but about 80 percent of the wetlands lost each year are in Louisiana.

Some loss of delta land is natural. About every thousand years, the river abandons its old winding, silt-filled path to take a shorter and steeper way to the ocean. Land sinks along abandoned channels. The delta builds where the water flows, and new sediment slowly clogs the channel. After a few thousand years, the sunken area around the abandoned channel offers a steeper route to the sea, and the river changes course again.

In 1904, the Army Corps of Engineers blocked one old and nearly abandoned channel. The present river channel is nearly a thousand years old, and the river is getting restless. The Atchafalaya River, which flows through an area that the river abandoned 3,800 years ago, now captures about 30 percent of Mississippi River water. All that keeps it from taking more is a flood-control structure built by the Army Corps of Engineers.

The delta now receives so little sediment that even the area around the active channel is sinking. In the Mississippi Delta, sea level is rising almost half an inch (1.2 centimeters) a year compared to the local land, five to ten times faster than global sea level. The problem had gotten little attention until recently because most of the lost land is sparsely populated marsh. Now state officials are trying to save the wetlands, which are important breeding grounds for birds, fish, and other marine creatures, and fertile fishing grounds. They also worry about losing money they now collect from oil and gas wells in the wetlands.

The Mississippi Delta may have the most severe problems, but some other river deltas around the world also are shrinking. The Aswân High Dam now captures sediments that would have kept the Nile River delta growing into the Mediterranean Sea. Dams in India trap silt from the Ganges River, which would have helped build the river delta in Bangladesh.

The Great Lakes

North America is a continent rich in lakes, with eight of the world's fourteen largest lakes. Lake Superior, which covers 31,700 square miles (82,100 square kilometers) between the United States and Canada, is the world's second-largest lake, and the largest containing fresh water. The four other Great Lakes also are among the world's fourteen largest, as are Great Slave Lake, Great Bear Lake, and Lake Winnipeg in Canada. All eight are new on the geological time scale; just eighteen thousand years ago, the sites of all of them were under thick ice sheets.

Stand on the shore of Lake Ontario, the smallest of the Great Lakes, and the lake almost looks like the ocean. The water seems endless; you can't see land on the other side. The lake has waves, although not as big as ocean waves, and a shore, although not as wide as an ocean beach. The waves are big enough to shape a shoreline and make some beaches, but the forces are much weaker than those of the ocean. The fierce winter storms on Lake Superior and Lake Huron have claimed many ships, but they cannot match the fury of a hurricane.

Ice sheets dug holes for the Great Lakes, and the holes started filling as the ice melted fifteen thousand to eight thousand years ago. Geologists tracing old beaches found that the Great Lakes started filling from the southern ends of Lake Michigan and Lake Erie as the glaciers retreated. The young lakes drained south, into the Mississippi. The ice melted slowly, eventually leaving the lakes looking almost as they look today. However, thousands of years ago, some water still trickled south from a place near present-day Chicago into the Mississippi. Water also flowed east from Lake Huron across Ontario, then through the present Ontario River into the St. Lawrence River. Today those paths are blocked, and water leaves the Great Lakes through Lake Erie and Lake Ontario.

What changed after the ice had melted? The land rose slowly when the weight of the ice was gone. It rose most in the north where the ice sheets had been thickest. Geologists have found old beaches formed five thousand years ago by the Great Lakes. Originally, they were all at the same level, but today old beaches near the northern tip of Lake Superior are about 700 feet (213 meters) above sea level, while those near Green Bay, Wisconsin, are only about 605 feet (184 meters) above sea level. The Canadian side of the lakes rose almost 100 feet (30 meters) more than the southern side since the melting of the ice. The southern boundaries of the Great Lakes have not changed much, but the old northern beaches were stranded high and dry.

Water levels in the Great Lakes, like those in other lakes, depend mainly on the heights of their outlets. Lake Superior is the highest, with water level 602 feet (183 meters) above sea level. A short river connects it to Lake Huron, which is joined to Lake Michigan; both are 580 feet (177 meters) above sea level. Lake Huron drains into Lake Erie, which is 572 feet (174 meters) above sea level, through two short rivers and the small Lake St. Clair near Detroit. Lake Ontario is much lower—246 feet (75 meters)—because it is below Niagara Falls.

Weather is important, however, and a series of wet or dry seasons can change water level by 6 feet (1.8 meters) in a little over a decade. When the Great Lakes were high in 1969, they eroded beaches and cliffs, damaging property along the shore. That change is much smaller than a hurricane storm surge, but much bigger than the change in sea level over the same period.

Great Salt Lake and the Caspian Sea

Great Salt Lake, the Caspian Sea, and the Aral Sea have three important things in common: They are landlocked lakes, with salty water in dry climates. The Caspian Sea, covering 143,000 square miles (370,000 square kilometers), is the world's largest lake; the Aral Sea is the fourth largest. (Despite their names, they are lakes because they are not connected to the ocean.) Great Salt Lake is far smaller and much shallower than either of the two larger lakes in the Soviet Union.

The levels of all three depends on climate. Rivers bring water that leaves steadily by evaporation. Heavy rains or snows swell the rivers, raising water level until it can evaporate. Evaporation continues when the weather is dry, so water level drops.

Water ran in the streets of Salt Lake City because rain and snow were heavy in Utah in the first half of the 1980s. The rivers added water to the shallow lake faster than evaporation could remove it. The area around the lake is flat, so the water spilled over a large area around the shore. The level was the highest since at least 1873, but it was much lower than it had been during the Ice Age. Utah was a much wetter place twenty thousand years ago, and its central valley was filled by a much larger lake, which geologists call Lake Bonneville. The old lake etched shorelines into the hills around the valley, and when it dried out, it left behind the Bonneville Salt Flats.

The Aral Sea has shrunk alarmingly since 1960, a pattern that will continue as long as large amounts of irrigation water are taken from the two rivers that feed the lake. In 1960, the Aral Sea covered 26,000 square miles (68,000 square kilometers); in 1987, it

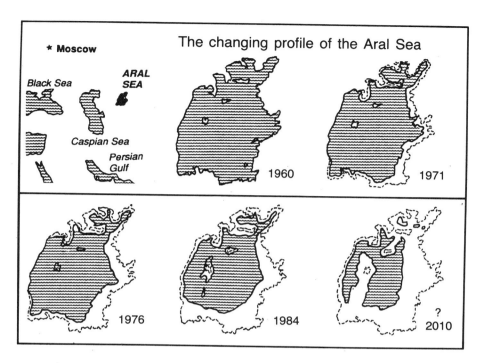

FIGURE 8–3: *The Aral Sea in the Soviet Union is shrinking because water is diverted from the rivers that feed it. (Courtesy of New Scientist magazine)*

covered only 16,000 square miles (41,000 square kilometers). The saltiness of the water has doubled, killing fish that had lived in the lake. Unless the Soviet Union takes drastic measures and releases more fresh water into the Aral Sea, Philip Micklin of Western Michigan University predicts it will continue shrinking, as shown in Figure 8–3, becoming "a lifeless residual brine lake" soon after the year 2000.

The Caspian Sea is in better condition because it is larger and much deeper, but it, too, is becoming saltier because less water is entering it.

9

Future Trends

The U.S. Geological Survey publishes a fascinating set of "topographic" maps, which plot in exacting detail the height of the land in the entire United States. A good local library should have a collection of them for your state, and perhaps for neighboring states as well. Lines on the maps connect points at the same height above sea level, as shown in Figure 9–1. Maps of small, flat areas may have contour lines every 5 feet above sea level; for larger, hillier areas, the contours may be every 50, 100, or 200 feet. If you learn to read these maps, you can see for yourself what changes rising sea level would bring.

We saw in Chapter 1 that the future trend in sea level is up. How much it rises depends on how much average global temperatures rise. The warmer the temperature, the more ice will melt from areas around the North and South poles, and the more seawater will expand, adding to the volume of the oceans. How much will temperatures rise? How much ice will melt? How much will sea level rise? Those are questions that scientists are still trying to answer.

Topographic maps let you ask "what if" questions. How much land would be flooded along the coast if sea level rose a certain amount? U.S. maps usually measure contours in feet, so you might look at sea levels 5, 10, 15, or 20 feet (1.5, 3, 4.6, or 6 meters) higher than today. If you live in Miami, New Orleans, or Galveston, the answers will scare you.

You can ask the same kind of questions about lake or river levels, which also appear on the maps. Look at topographic maps of Salt Lake City, and you can see why parts of the city were flooded when Great Salt Lake rose. Look at maps of St. Louis or New Orleans, and you can see why the cities have built dikes along the flood-prone Mississippi River.

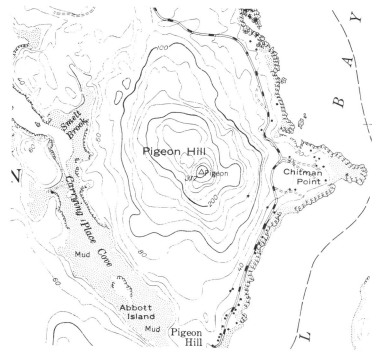

FIGURE 9–1: *A section of a topographic map of the Maine coast, with contours that show how far the land is above mean sea level. The bay at right is part of the Atlantic Ocean. Standard topographic maps are printed in color, with the contour lines brown, urban areas pink, water blue, and forests and grasslands green.*

Climate and Temperature Changes

Weather and temperature change all the time. Warm rain may follow a cold, clear day. Climate is the average weather, and we expect it to be more constant. No two New England winters are the same, but they differ from winters in North Dakota, Texas, or California.

Climate can change, although usually it takes many years. During the most recent ice age eighteen thousand years ago, northern Europe and North America were covered by thick ice sheets like those that cover Greenland and Antarctica today. The Washington, D.C., area was tundra just like areas of present-day Siberia or northern Canada. Rains fell and plants grew in the Sahara desert, and people lived there. Many millions of years ago, the earth had no polar ice caps, and the subtropical climate zone—now limited to the southern edge of the United States—reached as far north as Wyoming.

Climate is hard to measure, so scientists instead estimate average global temperature. They take their averages over many places and over the whole year to try to smooth out local variations. Figure 9–2 shows that these averages vary from year to year, but over a much smaller range than daily temperatures. Look carefully, and you can see that temperatures are headed up.

Current climate is not ideal, but major changes would cause big problems. Our civilization is built on assumptions about climate. We assume farmers can grow grain in the Midwest, but that could change with the climate. We assume sea level is constant, but climate could change that, too. If sea level changes, seaports might drown or be stranded above a shrunken ocean. Changes in temperatures and rain patterns could make it hard to grow crops in present farming areas, but possible to grow them farther north or south. People would see those changes as droughts and floods, and call them catastrophes. Scientists can see two different possibilities,

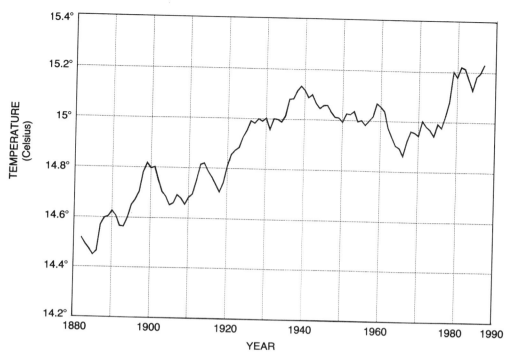

FIGURE 9–2: *Changes in average global temperature show a steady rise over the last hundred years. (Courtesy of Sergei Lebedeff, NASA Goddard Institute for Space Studies)*

a return to an ice age or global warming. Either extreme—a world with much larger ice caps or with little or no polar ice—would mean large changes in sea level.

Ice Ages

Temperatures in the tropics were not much colder during the ice age eighteen thousand years ago, but over the whole world temperatures averaged about 9° F (5° C) lower than today. The areas that were much colder were the temperate zones that cover most of Asia, Australia, Europe, and North America. Trees that grew in southern France during the ice age now grow near the Arctic Circle. Ice caps covered the sites of New York, Boston, Chicago, Minneapolis, Buf-

FIGURE 9–3: *Ice caps covered northern North America and Europe at the peak of the last ice age, 18,000 years ago. (From a drawing by A. Sotiropoulos in Ice Ages, by J. Imbrie and K. P. Imbrie, Enslow Publishers, Hillside, New Jersey.)*

falo, London, Moscow, and many other major cities. Canada and the Scandinavian countries (Sweden, Denmark, Finland, and Norway) were totally buried under ice, as shown in Figure 9–3.

The ice caps grew because for many years snow fell faster than it melted. Scientists believe that at their peak, those prehistoric ice caps contained three times more ice than now covers Greenland and Antarctica. The water that made the ice came from the oceans—so much water that sea level was about 280 to 330 feet (85 to 100 meters) lower than it is today. Much of today's shallow continental shelf was exposed along North America's Atlantic and Gulf coasts, as shown by the outer lines on Figure 9–4. Japan was a peninsula, connected to the Asian mainland. Large areas between Australia and southeast Asia were above sea level. Look carefully at

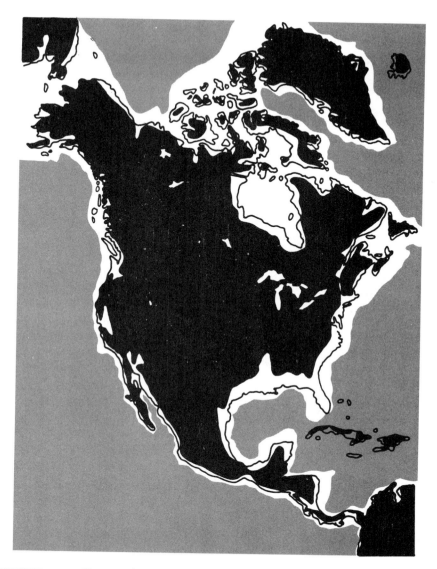

FIGURE 9–4: *During the peak of the last ice age, 18,000 years ago, much water was locked up in ice caps, and the lower sea level (shaded) exposed much of the continental shelf. The outline shows the present shore. If the ice caps melted and sea level rose another 200 feet (60 meters), only the dark part of North America would remain above water. (Courtesy of Edward J. Tarbuck and Frederick J. Lutkins, after R. H. Dott, Jr., and R. L. Battan)*

Figure 9–3, and you can see that Florida and the Bahamas were much larger than they are today and that Alaska was connected to Siberia.

Twenty or thirty years ago, many geologists thought the ice ages might return. The earth had spent most of the past million years in ice ages. Time and again the ice had advanced, then retreated during a brief "interglacial" period, only to advance again. The interglacials seemed only brief warm spells, lasting perhaps ten thousand years, between ice ages lasting one hundred thousand years. It looked like the ice was overdue to return.

Browse through a library, and you can still find books warning of the coming ice, and science-fiction novels set in futures where glaciers cover Manhattan. Scientists still believe that ice comes and goes in a natural cycle, but few of them worry about ice anymore. People have broken the ice cycle and started heating the globe.

Global Warming

The hot, dry summer of 1988 convinced many people in the United States that the world is getting warmer. Scientists know that one year can simply have unusual weather, so they do not consider one hot summer conclusive proof of global warming. However, global averages show that 1988 was the warmest year since accurate measurements began in the late 1800s. Just behind it are 1987, 1983, 1981, 1980, and 1986. You can see the trend in Figure 9–2; the world is getting warmer.

What is making the world warmer? Some scientists think natural cycles may play a role and that in time the climate may start cooling again. However, the leading suspect is people. We are releasing vast quantities of carbon dioxide into the atmosphere by burning fossil fuels such as oil, coal, and gas, and by clearing forests in the tropics. This carbon dioxide helps trap the sun's energy in the atmosphere by what is called the "greenhouse effect," because the same principle helps to keep greenhouses warm in winter. Before the 1988 summer heat wave, James Hansen of NASA's Goddard Institute for Space Sciences in New York told a congressional committee, "the greenhouse effect is here."

Carbon dioxide is a clear, odorless gas, which people and animals produce and which plants use in photosynthesis. Excluding water vapor, which varies in concentration, carbon dioxide is the fourth most common gas in the atmosphere. Air contains 78.080 percent nitrogen, 20.946 percent oxygen, 0.934 percent argon, and 0.034 percent carbon dioxide (abbreviated CO_2 because it contains one carbon atom and two oxygen atoms). What makes carbon dioxide special is how it helps the earth trap energy from the sun.

The sun's energy arrives as light, mostly at visible wavelengths around 20 millionths of an inch (0.0005 millimeter). Some of it is reflected from clouds, water, plants, and land, but most of it is absorbed. This solar energy heats the planet to what we consider reasonable temperatures—0° to 100° F (-18° to 38° C). At those temperatures, the earth itself emits energy as invisible infrared light at wavelengths twenty times longer, 400 millionths of an inch (0.01 millimeter). Most gases in the air let the infrared light through, but carbon dioxide absorbs it, so it cannot take energy into space, as shown in Figure 9–5. Thus, carbon dioxide helps keep the earth warm. (In addition to blocking infrared light, the glass in greenhouses keeps the warm air inside.) Without the carbon dioxide now in the atmosphere, the earth would be about 60° F (33° C) colder than it is now.

The problem is that the warming increases with the carbon dioxide level, and we are adding more of the gas to the atmosphere. Air preserved since 1850 contains only 0.029 percent carbon dioxide. By 1950, carbon dioxide level had reached 0.031 percent. The change has been getting faster, and by 1990 carbon dioxide may be 0.035 percent of the air—an increase of 20 percent since 1850 and over 10 percent since 1950.

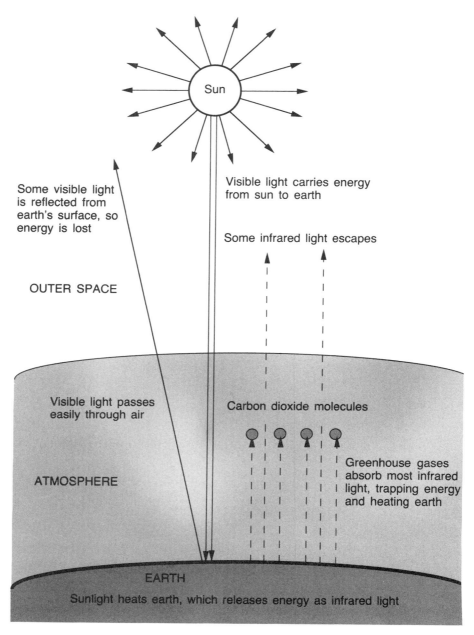

FIGURE 9–5: *The greenhouse effect warms the earth by blocking the escape of some of the sun's energy after it has been converted from visible light into infrared radiation.*

We know where the extra carbon dioxide is coming from. The biggest source is the burning of fossil fuels—coal, oil, and gas—that accumulated over hundreds of millions of years. Burning fuels cleanly generates carbon dioxide and water (improper burning releases even more harmful pollutants). In 1910, people burned enough fossil fuel to release about 4 billion tons of carbon dioxide to the atmosphere. By 1952, that total had doubled. It doubled again, to 16 billion tons, by 1970, and a few years later passed 20 billion tons.

Carbon dioxide also increases as people cut down trees, which normally remove carbon dioxide from the atmosphere. Wood from forests also releases carbon dioxide when it decays or burns, and bare ground returns more heat to the atmosphere than forests do. People removed Europe's forests long ago. Large areas of North American forest were felled from the 1600s through the 1800s, although some are now growing back. Today, people are felling tropical forests in South America, Asia, and Africa.

People also are adding other infrared-blocking "greenhouse" gases to the air. One is methane, which makes up a large part of natural gas. In 1850, air held only 0.9 part per million of methane. Today, it contains over 1.6 parts per million. Methane is part of the foul-smelling "marsh gas" produced when plants decay in swamps. Landfills make it, too, in a few cases enough to cause fires or explosions. Termites, cows, and rice paddies also make methane, and it is people who raise the cows and plant rice paddies. People also put synthetic chemicals called chlorinated fluorocarbons, or "CFCs," into the atmosphere. CFSs have gotten a lot of attention because they threaten the earth's protective ozone layer, but they also act as a greenhouse gas.

Scientists agree that greenhouse gases will raise temperatures, but they do not agree how much gases are being added, how much hotter it will get, or how that extra heat will change the weather. The National Academy of Sciences estimates that air's carbon dioxide content probably will double by 2100. The extra carbon dioxide itself may raise global temperature only 2° F (1° C), but other greenhouse gases and other effects would combine to make the total increase 3° to 8° F (1.5° to 4.5° C). That increase, in turn, would melt enough ice to raise sea level 1.6 to 11.5 feet (0.5 to 3.5 meters) by 2100.

With the smaller increase, coastal cities could buy time with bigger seawalls. The bigger increase threatens to drown low-lying cities like Miami and New Orleans. You may wonder why scientists cannot predict the increase any better. The reason is that weather and climate are incredibly complex, and even the most powerful supercomputers cannot predict them adequately. As the climate changes, cloud cover will change, and no one is sure how that will affect temperature.

Just to complicate things, nature also can add greenhouse gases to the air. Air preserved in Antarctic ice shows that carbon dioxide has varied between 0.018 percent and 0.030 percent over the last 150,000 years—long before people made any contributions beyond isolated campfires. The big increases came during warm interglacial periods about 130,000 and 18,000 years ago. The air contained the least carbon dioxide during the coldest periods, when ice sheets were largest. That makes sense if carbon dioxide helps warm the planet, but it doesn't tell us what caused the changes.

We know higher temperatures would raise sea level by melting ice, including mountain glaciers and the ice caps on Antarctica and Greenland. How much would melt? Scientists are not sure. The most vulnerable big ice sheets are those covering Greenland and western Antarctica (the side toward South America). If either one broke up, it could add about 20 feet (6 meters) of water to the oceans. Scientists believe that melting all the world's ice would raise sea level about 200 feet (60 to 70 meters). That would be enough to drown many important cities from Seattle to San Diego and from Miami to Portland, Maine, as shown in Table 9–1, as well as over

TABLE 9–1: *Major U.S. cities with downtown areas at altitudes under 50 feet. (Note that parts of these cities are at higher or lower altitudes.)*

City	Location	Altitude (feet)	(meters)
Albany, New York	inland	20	6.1
Atlantic City, New Jersey	Atlantic coast	10	3.0
Augusta, Maine	inland	45	13.7
Baltimore, Maryland	Chesapeake Bay	20	6.1
Bangor, Maine	inland	20	6.1
Beaumont, Texas	20 miles from Gulf of Mexico	20	6.1
Berkeley, California	San Francisco Bay	40	12.1
Biloxi, Mississippi	Gulf of Mexico	20	6.1
Boston, Massachusetts	Atlantic coast	21	6.4
Bridgeport, Connecticut	Long Island Sound	10	3.0
Camden, New Jersey	Delaware River	30	9.1
Charleston, S. Carolina	Atlantic coast	9	2.7
Corpus Christi, Texas	Gulf of Mexico	35	10.7
Daytona Beach, Florida	Atlantic coast	7	2.1
Eureka, California	inland	45	13.7
Galveston, Texas	island on Gulf of Mexico	5	1.5
Hartford, Connecticut	inland	40	12.2
Honolulu, Hawaii	Pacific coast	21	6.4
Houston, Texas	40 miles from Gulf of Mexico	40	12.2
Jacksonville, Florida	Atlantic coast	20	6.1
Key West, Florida	Atlantic coast/Gulf of Mexico	5	1.5
Long Beach, California	Pacific coast	35	10.7
Miami, Florida	Atlantic coast	10	3.0
Mobile, Alabama	Gulf of Mexico	5	1.5
New Haven, Connecticut	Long Island Sound	40	12.2
New Orleans, Louisiana	Mississippi River, near Gulf coast	5	1.5
Nome, Alaska	Bering Sea	25	7.6
Norfolk, Virginia	near Atlantic coast	10	3.0
Oakland, California	San Francisco Bay	25	7.6
Pensacola, Florida	Gulf of Mexico	15	4.6

City	Location	Altitude	
		(feet)	(meters)
Portland, Maine	Atlantic coast	25	7.6
Sacramento, California	inland	30	9.1
San Diego, California	Pacific coast	20	6.1
San Juan, Puerto Rico	Atlantic Ocean	35	10.7
Santa Cruz, California	Pacific coast	20	6.1
Savannah, Georgia	Atlantic coast	20	6.1
Seattle, Washington	Puget Sound	10	3.0
Stockton, California	inland	20	6.1
Tampa, Florida	Gulf of Mexico	15	4.6
Trenton, New Jersey	Delaware River	35	10.7
Washington, D.C.	Potomac River	25	7.6
Wilmington, N. Carolina	close to Atlantic coast	35	10.7

half of Delaware, Florida, Louisiana, and New Jersey. You can compile your own lists from topographic maps, atlases, and almanacs.

Impacts of Warming

What are the chances of all that ice melting? How long would it take? Many million years ago, the earth was warm enough that it did not have large polar ice caps. That does not mean it will be easy to melt the present ice caps. They did not melt completely during the last interglacial period 125,000 years ago, when sea level was higher than today. The main Antarctic ice sheet may be hard to melt because the continent sits at the South Pole. (Some scientists think the earth is cooler, and more likely to have glaciers, when a continent is at the pole.) There is so much ice it will take hundreds or perhaps thousands of years to melt. (The ice caps covering North America and Europe melted in thousands of years at the end of the ice age.) The water may rise quickly on a geological time scale, but not on a human scale.

Inland, far from the oceans, climate will change as temperatures rise, shifting climate and farming zones northward. The border between prairie and forest is now southwest of Minneapolis. It would move north about 30 to 50 miles for a one-degree Fahrenheit increase in average temperature (100 to 150 kilometers for each degree Celsius). If temperatures rise as much as some scientists expect, that border would move 300 miles (500 kilometers) north by 2030. Birds and animals can make the move, but trees will have problems. Some regions that now are fertile farming zones may dry out; others now too cold may warm up enough for farming. However, the details are hard to predict.

It is easier to predict how rising seas will change the coast. A 20-foot (6-meter) rise will dramatically shrink Florida, as shown in Figure 9–6. The Everglades will go first; large areas are no more than 5 feet (1.5 meters) above sea level. If sea level rises 15 feet (4.6 meters), Miami, the Keys, Fort Lauderdale, Daytona Beach, and Cape Canaveral will be underwater, and Lake Okeechobee will become part of the Atlantic. Higher seas will shrink the state even more; the state's highest point is 345 feet (105 meters) above sea level. Other coastal cities also are on a collision course with destiny. Raise sea level 15 feet (4.6 meters) and sightseers could tour colonial Boston with a rowboat. Melt all the ice and the ocean would come close to the tenth or fifteenth floors of New York City skyscrapers.

The End of Miami?

We can paint the picture in dramatic terms. Sea level has risen over 10 feet (3 meters)—something that could happen by 2100. Massive seawalls protect Miami Beach and metropolitan Miami from the Atlantic. To see the ocean, you must climb to the second or third floor of your hotel. The rising ocean long ago swamped the marshy Everglades, so barrier dikes on the west and south try to keep the salt water from flooding the lower western parts of the city.

Parts of the mainland are still above sea level, sandy ridges that parallel the old shoreline. Inland, much of the city is below sea level, although some streets have been raised to keep water pressure from buckling them. Pumps work overtime to keep seawater from seeping in through the sand. Drinking water is a problem. Heavy rains give city officials headaches because they put more burden on the pumps. The fortified city is the southernmost outpost of main-

FIGURE 9–6: *Melting the ice covering either Greenland or West Antarctica would raise sea level 20 feet (6 meters), drowning the dark areas, which are now above water. More ice melted during the last warm period between ice ages, 125,000 years ago, when the dotted areas were under water and Florida was a group of low islands. (Map by National Oceanic and Atmospheric Administration).*

land Florida. The ocean has drowned the highway to the few Keys that remain as outcrops barely above sea level, reachable only by boat and inhabited only by a few foolhardy souls who pray a hurricane will never come. The rising Atlantic has drowned many of the old routes north from Miami; only a handful are maintained.

The hurricane on its way from the mid-Atlantic will drench what is left of the Keys, but its center will pass over Biscayne Bay, the bull's-eye of the Miami area. Hurricanes are fueled by heat energy from the ocean, and warmer temperatures have helped hurricanes grow stronger than they were in the late 1900s. This one is a giant, packing winds near 200 miles an hour (320 kilometers per hour) as it sweeps across the Bahamas. Well over a million people jam routes north as they try to flee Miami and escape the storm. Some of them will not make it. The foolhardy stay behind, telling themselves that the city's billions of dollars of defenses will save them.

The storm hits at high tide, with a storm surge that easily tops the seawalls. Giant waves shatter the hotels and condominiums that tower along the shore. The entire city is flooded; salt water damages every structure left standing within its protective walls. Flood waters destroy the underground power grid and communication lines. The pounding of wind-driven waves wrecks most buildings near the coast. The pumps that kept the city dry die quietly in the storm, so the flood waters have nowhere to go.

Rescuers find thousands of survivors huddled in the ruins after the storm has passed. Concrete skeletons of houses and shattered condominiums stand in several feet of water trapped behind the seawall and the dikes. Damage is put at over $100 billion, and the death toll is over 100,000, but the devastation is so complete that no one can total the true costs. A few survivors vow to return, but as time passes no one will pay to rebuild the shattered city. The staggering amounts it would cost are needed to defend cities farther north along the Florida coast. New maps show a shorter Florida. The concrete remains of Miami and its seawalls collect sand, forming an island that seabirds visit until it is covered by the still-rising Atlantic.

Is this the fate that awaits Miami? The ingredients for the disaster are there. Miami Beach and Miami sit directly on the Atlantic coast, with only the Bahamas between them and the hurricanes that are part of life along the Atlantic coast. No one can be sure when the next big hurricane will hit, but the city has been very lucky to have missed the worst storms for more than fifty years. The highest points in Miami are ridges near the coast only about 20 feet (6 meters) above today's sea level. Go inland 5 miles (8 kilometers), and much of the land is only 5 to 10 feet (1.5 to 3 feet) above sea level. You have to go 150 miles (about 240 kilometers) from Miami before you reach land 100 feet (30 meters) above sea level. Yet about three million people live in the metropolitan area of Miami and Fort Lauderdale, making it the country's eleventh-largest metropolitan center.

Other Threatened Lands

Miami is not unique; it is only the most dramatic example. Houston is a little bigger, with over 3.5 million people, but its average altitude is 40 feet (12 meters) and it is not directly on the coast. New York City barely escaped the list of city centers below 50 feet (15 meters) in table 9–1; downtown Manhattan is 55 feet (16.8 meters) above sea level. Parts of many cities on the list are at higher altites, and some, such as Sacramento, California, and Albany, New York, are so far inland that a modest sea-level rise would not threaten them. But that does not change the basic problem.

We can extend the list of low-lying cities around the world. Downtown Sydney, Australia, is 25 feet (7.6 meters) above sea level. Both Tokyo and Rio de Janeiro have downtowns only 30 feet (9 meters) above sea level. Amsterdam and Rotterdam in the Netherlands are below sea level and depend on the Dutch dikes for their survival.

Rising sea level threatens nature, too. The Florida Everglades and the Louisiana bayous are unique wetland environments that lie mostly at no more than 5 feet (1.5 meters) above sea level. Thousands of square miles of Louisiana wetlands are within 3 feet (1 meter) of sea level.

You might think wetlands would simply reappear at what are today higher altitudes if sea level rises. As long as cliffs don't get in the way, the wetlands zone will move inland like a barrier island. However, in most areas the land slopes more above the marsh than the marsh itself does, so an increase in sea level will reduce the marsh area. Wetland areas may grow as water moves the silt, soil, and sand, but it will take many years.

If the Ice Caps Melt

It only took us 10 feet (3 meters) of sea level rise and a big hurricane to destroy Miami. What would happen if we melted the polar ice caps? The west Antarctic ice sheet would add about 20 feet (6 meters) to the oceans. Melting the rest of the world's ice caps would raise sea level about 200 feet (60 meters) above today's level.

You can see the consequences in Figure 9–4, where the dark inner part of the continent is what would remain. Virtually every city along the eastern coast of North America would drown. Only a stub of Florida's peninsula would remain. Southern New Jersey, Delaware, and coastal Maryland would be playgrounds for fish. The Mississippi River would have to start building a new delta in Arkansas. Houston, Corpus Christi, Washington, D.C., Baltimore, and Montreal would be underwater. On the western coast, the list includes Vancouver, British Columbia; Tacoma and Seattle, Washington; Portland, Oregon; Long Beach, Santa Barbara, San Diego, and

Oakland, California. The Pacific would turn much of California's central valley into a shallow sea, unless a huge barrier could be built across the Golden Gate at San Francisco.

The drowning would be worldwide. Leningrad, Amsterdam, and Copenhagen lie on coastal plains. A quick scan of the map shows many more low-lying cities: Tel Aviv, Israel; Alexandria in Egypt; Calcutta in India; much of Bangladesh; Singapore; Osaka; Tokyo; Shanghai; Hong Kong; and Buenos Aires. Measured in human terms, the damage would be enormous.

Could we build barriers against the sea? The Nurek Dam in the Soviet Union, the world's highest, is 1,000 feet (300 meters) tall. The Oroville Dam on California's Feather River is 754 feet (230 meters) tall, and many others are over 200 feet (60 meters) high. Yet these dams only block rivers; they run across valleys carefully chosen as the best sites. It would be much harder to build giant dams completely around a city to hold back the ocean. The ground on which the city sits might leak too much water for the giant dam to hold.

A walled city would not be a pleasant place to live. It would be a concrete canyon, with walls as high as 20-story buildings trying to hold out the ocean. Residents would have to watch day and night for water trying to seep through. They would have to watch more than just the giant dikes that surrounded the city. The tremendous pressure of the sea would continually try to push water up through the ground, and each tiny crack would threaten to become a massive gusher. And the cost of building and maintaining the giant walls would be immense.

10

Coastal Issues: Who Owns the Shore?

The signs along the beach come in many sizes, shapes, and forms, but they all carry the same message: PRIVATE PROPERTY: KEEP OFF. They may be nailed to fences, staked into the sand, or painted on walls. They may sit in front of shabby shacks or elegant 20-story condominiums. They appear along many shores, reminding us that individuals own most coastal land in the United States.

What you think of such signs depends on which side of the sign you're standing. If you're on the outside looking in, they are hostile barriers, promising some vague punishment if you dare cross the line. If you're on the inside looking out, they protect your property, keep out unwanted visitors, and maintain your privacy. Some people post signs only for legal reasons, to show that they own the shore or to discourage lawsuits if anyone is injured on the land; but others simply want to keep you out.

Whether or not you like them, private-property signs are a fact of life along the coast. They also are a fact of life in trying to deal with the shifting shore. Geologists know that the best thing for the beach is to let it retreat as sea level advances, but owners of coastal property don't want their houses to fall into the water. They might gladly let nature take its course on a national seashore, but they would rather build a seawall than have the rising sea devour their expensive lot. Trying to cope with coastal changes, like any other environmental issue, involves politics and social issues such as who owns the beach and what rights they have.

Public Lands and Parks

Federal, state, and local governments own much of the coast. The federal government maintains national seashores, parks, and wildlife refuges along the shore. Most are in wild areas, and most are open to the public, with some restrictions to prevent environmental damage. (The federal government also has some military bases on the coast, which are not open.) Many states have coastal parks, some wild and others developed for recreation. Resorts from Old Orchard Beach, Maine, to Santa Monica, California, own public beaches. Some limit access to residents or charge nonresidents stiff parking fees. Others open the beach to everyone, hoping to attract tourists.

Few resorts have unspoiled, or "natural," beaches. Shops, motels, cottages, or condominiums usually sit on the dunes. A bulkhead, revetment, or seawall may protect the buildings. A boardwalk may run along the beach, like the famous one in Atlantic City. Some small resorts have natural beaches, but they are often hard to find or far from major cities.

Local officials care about their beaches, but many view them more as resort attractions than as part of nature. Without the beach, the resort would be a poor town in trouble, like Cape May, New Jersey. Atlantic City; Ocean City, Maryland; and Miami Beach have spent millions of dollars to replenish their beaches with new sand. They want to preserve the beach and to protect the private property along the shore—the shops and hotels that cater to tourists. Caught between the rising sea and a hard place (the private property along the shore), resort towns try to "preserve" the beach by trapping sand with groins or adding new sand. Such beaches are more man-made than natural.

If you want to see the natural coast, visit state or national parks, or land owned by conservation groups such as the Nature Conservancy or the Audubon Society. Some state parks are managed like resort beaches for swimmers and sunbathers, but few of them have seawalls. Many parks are operated as natural and wildlife preserves, and human access is limited—sometimes in ways you don't notice. Paved roads, parking lots, and paths to the beach may be hard to find. At Plum Island National Wildlife Refuge in Massachusetts, rangers only admit as many cars as will fit in the modest parking areas. They turn people away once the parking areas are full.

The National Park Service manages national seashores for both conservation and recreation. Several bathhouses sit along the sandy bluffs overlooking the Atlantic on Cape Cod National Seashore, and lifeguards watch the crowded beaches below in the summer. However, those are the only places where stairs go down to the beach. Walk north or south from one of the crowded beaches and soon you are almost by yourself, with the sea on one side and the sandy cliffs on the other.

Park authorities usually let natural processes control the shore. That means that barrier beaches like Assateague Island National Seashore migrate inland, and the sandy bluffs erode on Cape Cod. Park officials refuse to build defenses, and let the sea claim parking lots, roads, and bathhouses. They know that the beach will remain after it moves.

Historic coastal buildings like the Cape Hatteras Lighthouse do pose problems for the parks. Should they preserve the coastline or the building? The best solution, according to coastal geologists, is to move the lighthouse back from the shore and let erosion claim the original site.

"Save Our Homes"

Park officials can let their own buildings fall into the sea, but things are different when the building falling into the water is someone's home. As the seas rise, the ocean threatens private property as well as parkland. When a home is at stake, the result can be a little drama like the one played out in Chatham, Massachusetts, in early 1988.

In January 1987, a northeaster broke through Nauset Beach, the sandy spit that protected Chatham Harbor from the sea. Water level rose 1 foot (0.3 meter) in the harbor, and strong waves hit the shore. Not much happened that spring and summer, but from September 1987 until January 1988, parts of the coast eroded about 100 feet (30 meters). Houses had been built there fifty years earlier, and home owners worried as the ocean relentlessly approached their doorsteps. On January 21, 1988, the $400,000 summer home of a retired New Jersey judge, built in 1938, fell into the water, as shown in Figure 10–1. The ocean devoured part of a town parking area. Owners of the remaining homes dumped rocks on the beach, trying to stop the ocean.

The story was a regular feature on the front page of Boston newspapers. "Save our homes," shouted residents, demanding protection for their property. State officials denied most of the requests. The state's 1978 Wetlands Preservation Act banned building revetments or seawalls along coastal dunes or bluffs, because that would cut off sand supplies needed by other parts of the beach. A few homes fell under an exception, because they were built on bluffs before the law went into effect. There was no exception for houses built on dunes. Home owners took state officials to court.

Some newspaper stories portrayed state officials as heartless bureaucrats, unwilling to save threatened homes. State geologists denied the charge. They explained that protecting part of the shore would only speed erosion elsewhere, by cutting off the supply of

FIGURE 10–1: *Erosion claims a house in Chatham, Massachusetts. The ocean had eroded about 100 feet of the coast in the five months before the picture was taken in January 1988. (Photo by Stephen Heaslip,* Cape Cod Times)

sand that kept other beaches from eroding. They added that much of the eroded land was dunes that the sea had deposited before the houses were built. They said the houses should never have been there and brought old maps to show a 140-year cycle of erosion and land building in Chatham Harbor. Old records indicated that homes had been built in the same spot in the 1800s, only to fall into the harbor during an earlier erosion cycle.

By February 1989, Chatham had lost eight more homes to the Atlantic, and town officials were still debating what to do about the problem. The drama had stopped making headlines in the Boston papers, but coastal geologists warned that more trouble could be on the way. Coastal geologist David Aubrey of the Woods Hole Oceanographic Institution predicted another break in the barrier islands along southern Cape Cod, this one opposite the town of Orleans, just north of Chatham. There it would expose more expensive homes to strong currents and heavy erosion. Those houses are not alone. Massachusetts officials say that waves from a heavy storm could attack over one thousand more buildings on Cape Cod.

Should coastal property be protected? The decision is a tough one. Americans traditionally put great value on their homes. "Save our homes" is an emotional cry that brings sympathy. Yet what should we do if the house was built in the wrong place? Can we afford to defend every house threatened by the rising ocean? The cost of defending the six houses sitting on the Chatham bluffs was estimated at $300,000 to $400,000—over $50,000 each. Worse yet, stopping erosion from that area would stop sand from reaching other parts of the shore. That would speed erosion in those places, creating new problems and the need for more defenses. Residents ask why they weren't warned of such problems. State officials respond that geologists did not understand how erosion worked when the houses were built.

Money is a big part of the issue. When the waves come crashing toward a house, the owner gladly offers to do anything he or she can to save it, including spending tens of thousands of dollars for a seawall. But when the time comes to pay the bill, the owner looks for help from the government. In some cases, defenses may cost more than the property they are supposed to protect.

Local, state, and federal governments have long helped develop the shore in many ways. Local and state governments build roads and provide water and sewer service. The federal government sponsors flood insurance that pays people for damages to their coastal property. State and local governments pay for work that makes beaches more attractive, such as adding new sand. In the past, governments also have paid for seawalls and other coastal defenses.

This has changed recently as government officials have learned more about erosion. Many states restrict new development along the coast. The federal government has stopped helping coastal developers. It has changed the flood insurance program so it pays to move homes back from the ocean and will not cover homes built too close to the water.

State and local governments find themselves in the midst of the old dispute between private-property rights and the public good. Owners of coastal homes like those in Chatham believe that the town should pay to defend their property, because the town taxes them on that land. Other people believe that coastal defenses would cost too much or would only benefit a few wealthy property owners. Many geologists argue that defenses are futile as well as expensive, and that they will only speed destruction of unprotected beaches. Some of the same issues arise when developers and owners of coastal property are willing to pay for their own defenses, because those defenses can hurt other beaches.

The Human and Economic Stakes

Part of the problem with coastal development is that we have emotional ties to our homes. We want our houses to be safe havens and not vulnerable to acts of fate or catastrophes like storms and floods. Many people risk money on foolish things, but few would risk gambling their homes on a toss of the dice.

The ocean shore is a fascinating and beautiful place, but rising sea level, storms, and erosion make living there a gamble. People have known that for thousands of years. The ancient Greeks told legends of the sunken land of Atlantis, which have intrigued scholars for centuries. (The legends give few details, but they may have been based on a volcanic eruption that destroyed an island in the Aegean Sea.) Even the Bible warns of the danger of building on sand.

Until the twentieth century, most people heeded those warnings. America's nineteenth-century ports lay in protected harbors or near river mouths. The site of New Orleans was the highest ground avail-

able for a port near the mouth of the Mississippi when the governor
of Louisiana founded the city in 1718. It wasn't high enough, and
within ten years residents had to build a levee to keep the river out
of the town, but it shows that early settlers worried about flooding.
The port of San Francisco lies protected inside the Golden Gate on
San Francisco Bay; cliffs, not docks, face the Pacific Ocean.

Today, people erect large buildings on the shore, blithely assum-
ing that modern engineering can protect them from disaster. There
is poetic justice in the fact that the state of New Jersey has turned
its most famous coastal resort, Atlantic City, over to the gamblers.
In a casino, some bettors win, but the odds are set so the only sure
winner is the "house"—the owners of the casino itself. In the same
way, the odds in the game of building along the coast are stacked in
favor of the sea. People may win their coastal gambles for a while—
perhaps even for a lifetime. Yet as the water rises, the storm risk
grows, and the sea stands to hit the jackpot when the dice of fate
come up showing "hurricane" or "nor'easter."

The financial stakes today are gigantic. Property worth hundreds
of billions of dollars lie along the North American seacoast. Erosion
is eating some of it. Hurricane Hugo did over three billion dollars in
damage to South Carolina in 1989. Less powerful storms can cause
millions of dollars in damage overnight. The odds get worse as the
sea rises.

There are human stakes as well, for millions of people live along
the coast. They are threatened not by the slow rise of the sea but by
the random attacks of storms. The storm warnings we take for
granted today were not available before World War II. Even today's
warnings arrive only a day before the hurricane; we cannot predict
the storm's path days in advance. People need time to evacuate the
threatened coast, especially the many elderly people in beachfront
condos. Look at a map of any barrier island town and you can see
the problem. A highway runs the length of the island; but there
usually are only one or two bridges to the mainland. If those become

jammed, they can trap people on the island. Many of the six thousand people who died in the Galveston hurricane might have lived if they had gotten off the island before the bridges were blocked.

Too many people ignore storm warnings. Some decide to stay home because storms missed them before. They might be lucky again, or they might share the fate of the people at the party for Hurricane Camille in Pass Christian, Mississippi. Too many forget that even our modern technology can underestimate storms.

11

Options for the Shifting Shore

Most Americans do not know that sea level is rising, or think that the changes are too small to matter. It is tempting to put off dealing with a change in sea level that—at present—averages only a tenth to a twentieth of an inch (2.4 to 1.2 millimeters) a year around the world. However, that easy course is a dangerous one. A small rise in sea level can push the shore back a much larger distance. Sea level could soon rise faster, and some land is sinking even faster than the sea is rising. We need to take a long, hard look at the choices available.

We have three basic ways to attack the problem of rising sea level:

- Try to stop the increase before it happens.
- Defend the coast against rising sea level.
- Retreat from threatened land.

There probably is no single solution that is best for the entire coast. Each approach has its attractions and limitations. Those that sound the best usually are the most difficult.

136

Stopping Global Warming

If we are to stop the worldwide rise in sea level, we must stop the trends that are warming the whole planet. That sounds like a good idea, because it could attack the problem of climate change as well. However, it means we must find ways to control the release of greenhouse gases like carbon dioxide and methane. That is a much harder problem than controlling the release of other pollutants, because perfectly clean burning of wood, coal, oil, or gas produces carbon dioxide.

We can slow the release of carbon dioxide in many ways. We can use energy more efficiently, so we need to burn less fossil fuels. We can shift from fossil fuels to renewable energy sources such as solar power, wind power, and water power. We can consider nuclear power, which has serious problems but which does not produce greenhouse gases. However, we must remember there are many, many ways we add carbon dioxide to the atmosphere. Cars and home furnaces make carbon dioxide, so we must drive less and heat our homes less. Other sources are cooking fires in developing countries, gas stoves in our kitchens, barbecue grills in our backyards, and a list that goes on almost forever.

We might try to control carbon dioxide emissions at the source, but this would work best for power plants. It would be virtually impossible—and incredibly expensive—to collect carbon dioxide from every car or home heater and convert it into something harmless.

Trees and other plants collect carbon dioxide and release it when they die. The clearing of tropical forests is adding carbon dioxide to the air, and stopping that clearing would help ease the warming problem. We also could plant new trees, which could absorb excess carbon dioxide after it is released into the air. However, the new trees would have to cover vast areas, and they could solve only part of the problem.

It is important to seek ways to slow or stop global warming, but the problem is a difficult one that at best will be very expensive to attack. The most we can hope for for many years is to slow down the rate of increase, not to stop it or reverse it. This may slow the rise of sea level, but it will not stop it. Nor will it help problems caused by the settling of land, which causes most land loss in Louisiana and contributes to erosion elsewhere.

The Case for Defense

If we can't stop the rising sea, can we at least defend against it? Defenses have worked in the past. After Galveston was devastated by the 1900 hurricane, the city invested $1.6 million in a seawall and $2 million in 12 million cubic yards (9 million cubic meters) of fill to raise the city higher above the sea. When the next hurricane hit, in 1915, only twelve people died in Galveston, and property damage was only one-fifth that in the earlier storm. The Dutch have defended their country from the sea for over a thousand years; today they have massive dikes like the one shown under construction in Figure 11–1. All around the world, threatened cities owe their existence to seawalls, bulkheads, and groins. Beach replenishment has worked well to rebuild beaches in places like Miami Beach, although the new sand has not lasted long on some other beaches.

Advocates of defenses doubt that sea level will rise rapidly. They point to historical records indicating a rise of only 4.7 inches (12 centimeters) in the last hundred years, although new research indicates the actual rate may be twice as fast. They also insist that such a small rise could not overwhelm massive defenses.

The biggest reason to defend the coast is money. Many billions of dollars are invested in coastal property, from cities such as New York and Seattle to resorts like Daytona Beach and Fort Lauderdale. Tourist, resort, fishing, and shipping industries have built up around the sea. It is hard to walk away from all that money and from the

FIGURE 11–1: *Building a dike, like this one off the Dutch coast, is a massive undertaking. (Courtesy of Royal Netherlands Embassy)*

dreams many people have of living along the coast. Defenses promise to preserve those investments and dreams.

However, defenses are far from perfect. They must be maintained and upgraded as sea level rises. No defense can provide perfect protection from a direct hit by a severe storm. Coastal armaments can speed erosion of other parts of the shore and of the beach below the defenses. Too large an increase in sea level might make defenses impractical, although we do not know where to draw that line.

Finally, defense costs a lot of money. Holland spent $12 billion on its new defenses against the North Sea, not counting maintenance. The United States has 26,700 miles (43,000 kilometers) of shoreline on the Atlantic Ocean and 17,100 miles (27,500 kilometers) on the Gulf of Mexico. The Pacific shore is 40,300 miles (64,800 kilometers) long, more than three-quarters in Alaska, which also has 2,500 miles (4,000 kilometers) of shore on the Arctic Ocean. If we neglect Alaska, that still adds up to some

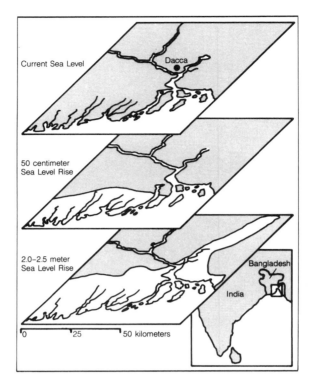

FIGURE 11–2: *A 20-inch (50-centimeter) rise in sea level would submerge large areas where people live in Bangladesh. A rise of 6.6 to 8.2 feet (2 to 2.5 meters) would be disastrous. (Courtesy of United National Environment Program)*

50,000 miles (80,000 kilometers) of shore. At $5 million per mile, building simple seawalls around the country would cost $250 billion and would protect only against a small rise in sea level.

The high costs of defenses make them out of the question for poor countries. Like Holland, much of Bangladesh is low-lying river delta. Figure 11–2 shows how a small rise in sea level could submerge large areas in Bangladesh, which desperately needs the fertile land to feed its growing population. However, while Holland is an affluent country, Bangladesh is one of the world's poorest nations. It has no way to afford the massive defenses it would need to keep out the Indian Ocean.

The Attractions of Retreat

Only a foolish general refuses to think of retreat. It is the only sensible thing when an army faces a much stronger force. Many coastal geologists believe it is the only sensible thing to do when facing the rising sea.

Their idea of retreat is not to abandon the shore, but to move back a safe distance. If the sea threatens to destroy a building, they would rather move the structure away from the water than armor the coast with a seawall. They urge that new buildings be set far enough back from the water so that many years of erosion will not threaten them. They want to stop challenging nature by building on the water's edge—and start living with how nature shapes the shore.

As long as the oceans are rising, they will push natural shores inland in front of them. Trying to stop this motion will destroy the beach. Many coastal geologists also argue it will be futile in the long run, because the sea has enough power to destroy all of our defenses. Advocates of retreat also say it is the only rational economic course, because defending the entire coast would be incredibly expensive.

Deciding to retreat from the shore does mean sacrifices. Some are economic. Buildings built too close to the ocean may have to be abandoned, and property values will drop because the land is no longer suitable for building. Others are more emotional, like abandoning the dream of "a little place along the shore" where you could vacation or retire. Those kinds of sacrifices may be the hardest to make.

Retreat is not an option for a few countries that occupy low-lying islands. No point in Tuvalu, a tiny country made up of nine islands in the southwest Pacific, is more than 15 feet (4.6 meters) above sea level. The Maldives, a chain of over 1,000 small islands southwest of India, also is flat and very low. Residents of those countries have nowhere to retreat from rising sea level.

New Policies

New government coastal policies include retreat as well as engineering. New rules require new buildings to be set back from eroding shores, existing buildings to be moved to safer spots, and coastal development to be discouraged. They try to strike a balance between man and nature. "I'm convinced more and more that there's no one answer," said Jeff Benoit of the Massachusetts Office of Coastal Zone Management, after the first house fell into the ocean at Chatham. The state limits new development along the shore, but will not abandon downtown Boston or the city's airport, both of which are built on lowland along Boston Harbor.

In North Carolina, small buildings now must be set back far enough from the shore that erosion will take at least thirty years to reach them. Large buildings must be set back twice as far from the shore, so they can survive for at least sixty years. The state also bans new bulkheads, groins, and seawalls. The rules took effect in 1979, but about 750 older buildings could fall into the ocean in the next decade even without a major storm.

New buildings on sand dunes and beaches in Maine can cover only 20 percent of the lot area. The state also bans new buildings more than 35 feet (11 meters) high—about three stories. However, a few developers got in under the wire, and taller buildings were being finished in Old Orchard Beach in the summer of 1988.

State and town rules differ widely. Some have followed the leads of Maine, Massachusetts, and North Carolina and limit building on the coast. Other states, such as New Jersey and Texas, have few limits. High-rise condominiums were built near the surf in Myrtle Beach, South Carolina, in time for their ground floors to be ruined by Hurricane Hugo in 1989. Another condominium complex stands—at the moment—at the west end of the Galveston seawall, where the erosion rate is 15 feet (4.6 meters) a year.

National parks, seashores, and wildlife refuges are left natural; the

National Park Service avoids defenses and lets their shores retreat naturally. In 1972, the federal government passed the Coastal Zone Management Act, which helps pay for long-term state programs to manage the coasts of the oceans and the Great Lakes. Most of the thirty-five eligible states participate. A 1982 law put undeveloped barrier islands, spits, and dunes on the East and Gulf coasts into the Coastal Barrier Resource System. The federal government will not pay to aid building on this land, which means there is no money to build roads and bridges, and no federal flood insurance.

In 1988, the National Flood Insurance Program, which covers about $160 billion in property, changed its rules to encourage retreat from the coast. Like other insurance programs, it had paid people only if their property was destroyed. That meant people could only collect insurance on coastal buildings if they fell into the water. The new rules pay home owners up to 40 percent of the house's value if they move it far enough from the shore to survive thirty years of erosion. Bigger buildings must be moved back even farther. If a building declared in "imminent danger" can be moved and is not moved, its owner can collect only 40 percent of the insured value if the building is left in place and destroyed by the sea. This will not penalize home owners like those in Chatham who had no place to move, but for the first time it uses insurance to reduce losses before they happen.

Future Uncertain

Scientists are looking closely at the problems presented by rising sea level. An urgent need, said a panel of the National Academy of Sciences, is to improve future predictions of sea level, which now have a large range of uncertainty. Their 1987 report warned people planning projects along the coast that they "should consider the high probability of accelerated sea-level rise." The panel did not say how much change was likely, but cited estimates ranging from 1 to

11.5 feet (0.3 to 3.5 meters) by the year 2100. That's a lot of uncertainty.

The panel concluded that the rises in sea level "should not be a cause for alarm or complacency." However, some coastal geologists are more worried. Many beaches along the Atlantic and Gulf coasts have been lined with condos since the last hurricane struck. The United States was lucky to miss Hurricane Gilbert in 1988, one of the most intense storms on record. The storm left 500,000 people homeless in Jamaica and caused $880 million in damage to Mexico. Hurricane Hugo in 1989 was not quite as powerful, but it caused over three billion dollars in damage to South Carolina. No one knows when the next big hurricane may hit a city like Miami or New Orleans, or a heavily developed coastal area like Fort Lauderdale or Daytona Beach, but we do know that hurricanes will come again.

As sea level rises, the storm threat grows. As years pass without a major storm, memories fade. People settle along the coast who know nothing of hurricane dangers. New buildings rise where storms destroyed others. More elderly people—perhaps your grandparents among them—retire to the shore to enjoy sand and sun. Cities and towns along the coast grow, and developers try to satisfy the demand by building more homes and condos. Beaches shrink, leaving less sand to absorb the energy of storm waves. We risk growing too confident of defenses that cannot be tested until the full fury of a storm is upon us. All the while, sea level inches higher.

The future of the coast is uncertain, but we know the shore will continue shifting, retreating inland as the earth warms and sea level rises. We cannot be certain how much warmer the earth will get or how much sea level will rise, any more than we can be sure where the next hurricane will strike. We can armor the coast, but we know that seawalls can fail. We must balance our desire to live along the shore against the costs and risks, and try to limit the damage.

Many coastal geologists urge strategic retreat from the ocean. In

1985, a group headed by geologist James D. Howard of the Skidaway Institute of Oceanography in Savannah, Georgia, conservationist Wallace Kaufman of Pittsboro, North Carolina, and Orrin H. Pilkey, Jr., of Duke University warned: "Sea level is rising and the American shoreline is retreating. We face economic and environmental realities that leave us two choices: Plan a strategic retreat now or undertake a vastly expensive program of armoring the coastline and, as required, retreating through a series of unpredictable disasters."

Even the staunchest advocates of retreat say that defenses have their place, to protect big cities along the coast. "It might be worth spending a lot of money to save Manhattan, but not Carolina Beach, North Carolina," says Pilkey. The problem becomes where to draw the line. Should we try to save Miami? New Orleans? Charleston, South Carolina? Atlantic City?

How long can we save coastal cities if sea level continues rising? In Chapter 9, we saw how a hurricane could destroy Miami if sea level rose 10 feet (3 meters). It might take a larger increase, but if the sea does not stop rising, it someday will overwhelm any defenses we can build around Miami long before we run out of ice to melt.

What will the future bring? Will the sea chase us inland, creating seaports in Arkansas and drowning most of Delaware and Florida? Will armored cities sit miles offshore, surrounded by giant dikes and ocean waters far above the city streets? Or will we find a way to balance our way of life with the needs of the planet? The answers to those questions are up to all of us.

Index